Best wishes,
Nicki Royall Peet

W9-BWG-176

THE
Shaman's
DAUGHTER

A Novel

NICKI ROYALL PEET

iUniverse LLC
Bloomington

THE SHAMAN'S DAUGHTER

iUniverse books may be ordered through booksellers or by contacting:

iUniverse
1663 Liberty Drive
Bloomington, IN 47403
www.iuniverse.com
1-800-Authors (1-800-288-4677)

ISBN: 978-1-4917-2208-4 (sc)
ISBN: 978-1-4917-2210-7 (hc)
ISBN: 978-1-4917-2209-1 (e)

Library of Congress Control Number: 2014901179

Printed in the United States of America.

iUniverse rev. date: 01/31/2014

To my grandsons, Raleigh, Jackson, and Owen—
may you always have the courage of your convictions.

Contents

Acknowledgments

*M*uch gratitude to my husband, Cary, for his patience and support in the writing of *The Shaman's Daughter.* Also, many thanks to my daughters, Hagen and Samantha, for their support—especially to Samantha for her help with editing and proofreading. Gratitude as well to all my wonderful family and friends who encouraged me along the way.

The Cherokee Creation Story: Water and Fire

*J*n the beginning of time, all animals lived in the Galun Lati, the sky vault. They lived on a giant rock but were very crowded there. Below, everything was water. They couldn't live well on water, and they wondered what was underneath the water. Maybe there was land there they could inhabit, so they could spread out a little.

Finding nothing to support them on the water's surface, the smallest among them, the water beetle, dove down to see if he could find anything useful below. When the water beetle arrived at the bottom, he discovered wet mud, which he brought back to the top. Eventually the wet mud started to expand, and after a time, it became the island called earth.

The great buzzard, sent from Galun Lati, checked on how well the land was drying out. He had landed in Cherokee country to rest and flap his wings. Since the earth was still damp, he shaped many mountains and valleys.

After the land was dry, the rest of the animals came down to occupy it. They set the sun in motion across the sky. Each corner of the earth was held on top of the water by thick cords attached to the sky vault at it strongest points.

The small water spider was the only creature to succeed in bringing back fire from a stump struck by lightning. All the big animals had tried to retrieve the fire. The raven, the screech owl, the horned owl, and the black snake had all taken a shot at it. In the process, all had been severely burned.

But the water spider succeeded and brought back a single coal of fire in its *tusti* bowl. The world has had fire ever since.

PART 1

Cistoo's Journey

Chapter 1

The Shaman

The sound could be heard over three mountains, which is a far distance: three days to walk on foot. Yet the sound of the bird's music floated fast and easy on the air. It was the morning song of a whip-poor-will. Letodah's job was to search for a certain green plant in the woods. He stopped every few hours to blow his small pipe to alert the tribe that he had kept to his mission. He also used this occasion to touch and kiss the amulet around his neck, which gave him strength and direction. The necklace identified him as the tribe's shaman.

Finding this special fern would be hard. Four or five other plants resembled it, but none of the others would cure the child's ailment. In fact, the others could make the child sicker. Letodah took great care to detect the special green plant. It grew low to the ground near the base of cedar trees and had a red tinge around the edges. When soaked in hot water, the leaves became a medicinal drink. The liquid would ward off the nightmares and delirium haunting the sick girl.

Only six years on the earth, she had lived much of it ill. She had pulled through earlier bouts of fever, chills, and delirium, but Letodah doubted she would live this time.

He was aware of the shadows of the day growing longer, yet he knew he must continue searching. The village was counting on him. He was their medicine man. He danced for the sick. He knew the right recipes and proportions to use when cooking the healing potions. In a self-induced trance, he had traveled to the Underworld for his people. He located their demons, returned their angels to them, and sometimes even retrieved their souls.

Letodah remembered the story passed down from his ancestors about the great sickness that had wiped out nine out of ten Cherokees a hundred years earlier. The Indians suspected that the illness had come with the arrival of the European colonists. Many early settlers had died from the same diseases that later killed the Indians. The diseases had eventually spread inland. Letodah wondered if the harsh illness Cistoo suffered could be a remnant of the white man's curse.

So the uninvited settle on land that is not theirs and spread sickness. The thought of it gave him energy to run faster and search harder.

Letodah recognized the sound of the whip-poor-will wafting from his village. He wished he were back there. But he could not go back. He would not go back until he had found this herb. He looked in all the places where he expected to find it—places where he had plucked it in the past—but it was nowhere to be found.

He walked deeper into the woods at the base of Grandfather Mountain.

A crowd of cedars lies ahead that may have plantings, he thought.

After falling to his knees on the ground before the big trunks, he searched carefully at their bases for even the smallest sprout. He paused for only a moment to drink water from his pouch and to rip a piece of dry deer meat from his belt. He would run out of food soon. He could hunt for more, but that too would take time.

He began the search again, crawling from tree to tree, investigating the green sprouts between the above-ground

4

roots. At last he came to a thin tree that he was tempted to pass by. But a large clump of the herb emerged from its base with apparent abandon.

He pulled all of it up out of the earth and said, "Thank you, medicine, for your life and for the life you will save." After cramming the leaves and roots into his bag, he ran swiftly through the woods toward the sound of the whip-poor-will.

Back in camp, the child's mother, Nannuht, could barely sit. Her body ached from lack of sleep. She used all of her energy to remain upright. For days, she had stayed awake, watching and caring for her daughter. The small girl had been sick for many days. Her head grew hot and then cold every night. Her body shook. Her mother barely managed to make her sip small amounts of water. Nannuht's face looked desperate, like a fox caught in a trap, a fox that had gnawed its leg to a stub only to realize that the other leg was trapped too, with no way to free it. Nannuht was trapped by what she saw as an inevitable grief.

The time is close, she thought, *when Cistoo won't need me to take care of her anymore.* Her daughter's death might bring temporary relief to her. The relief might last long enough for her to nod off for a few seconds. But whatever relief she might experience would not last long. She would awaken fully and fitfully to another resurfacing blow of grief. Grief would stick by her, whispering the news in her ear: *She's lost. She's never coming back.*

Cistoo had woken up screaming in the night. "The wolf, the wolf," she yelled. "Stop, chasing me, stop!" This was the same dream Cistoo had often told her mother. The wolf stalked her, appearing around every tree, even as she ran.

Cistoo moaned. It was morning. Her body drenched in sweat, Nannuht removed the deerskins and covered her daughter with dry oak leaves to absorb the moisture. The leaves would cool and soothe the child.

Letodah must come back soon. Nannuht thought. *He must.*

She placed four rocks on the ground each pointing to a separate spirit of the four directions. She lit sage and smudged her daughter's head with the ashes.

"See me, with your mind's eye, returning to camp with the medicine," Letodah had said when he told her to follow these practices while he was gone. In that way he could be present to guide her through the worst of the illness.

Letodah felt the wind to his back. His black hair flew behind him as he ran. His flat features flattened even more from the air's pressure. *Spirit of the wind, push me along,* he prayed. *Push me fast. Make me arrive in time.* His long legs had grown muscular from the distances he ran each morning to stay strong for his work.

To Letodah, death was not the opposite of life. Death was the view from another plane. Death and life were not separate. Both contained seeds of one another. Each revealed what the other could not.

He ran because it was his work and because he had a vision. It was his life.

He could see the village ahead: the circle of huts with smoke rising from their centers. The braves had constructed a vertical log fence around the perimeter to add an extra measure of safety to the inhabitants. Even though big trees appeared ahead of him, he ran around them easily, as if they had stepped aside to accommodate him. Barely slowing down, he ran through streams and remained upright.

He did not hear. The only sound he heard was the sound in his mind, the last sound he had heard before going on the healing journey. He heard the sound of the girl's screams and moans. He saw her mother's pleading eyes.

As he drew closer to the village, the night fires were dying out. It was shortly before dawn. From the mountainside, he could see the glowing embers of the inner circle fire and knew he was close to home.

I know I will find the girl alive, but just barely, his intuition told him.

Letodah collapsed, exhausted, next to the pallet where Cistoo lay. Her wet hair from the broken fever was matted to her head. Her mother sat next to her, and she was sleeping too, sitting up. Nannuht startled awake when Letodah arrived. The slight rush of wind and leaves as he kneeled had frightened her.

Immediately, he began to prepare the plant over the fire in a small bowl that Nannuht provided for him. The girl lay hot and flush, her body limp and unmoving; she breathed shallowly and very slowly.

The water mixed with the plant brewed for a while until some special time of Letodah's knowing. Then it was ready. "The potion must cool a little so Cistoo's lips will not be burned," Letodah said as his large hand carefully lifted the girl's head from the folded blanket. "I want her to swallow it without choking."

She could take only small sips at a time. This had been the problem for days. Her frame was no more than skin and bony protrusions.

Letodah could see Nannuht's frustration as she watched him force her daughter to down the drink. *This must seem useless to Nannuht,* Letodah thought. He saw Nannuht's eyes shut. Apparently, she had just enough strength left in her to observe Cistoo take the medicine. She hung on a while longer before sleep overtook her. Letodah knew that she had been nursing her child for days with little thought of herself. *Let her sleep,* Letodah thought. *For now, there is nothing more she can do.*

After Letodah forced Cistoo to swallow the whole potion, he lay down next to her to go on a spirit journey. He would enter the Underworld, where the spirits could carry away this sickness to a distant spot. He took the sickness unto himself as if it were a parcel on his sash. *I will find a place for it in the Underworld far away from Cistoo, where it can harm no one.*

As a shaman, he knew this was the place where he faced the biggest danger. Because he had taken the sickness unto himself, it could stick to him and overtake him. He must find a good container for it.

He was not afraid of death. Death showed him how to live. He was always aware of it. They were old friends.

Letodah roamed in the Underworld with his sparrow guide before locating a spot to leave the sickness. The spot where he laid it generated great power and compassion. A wide gap in a rock cracked open to receive the disease and immediately shut back up. The strength of this place was so big that the sickness would be enfolded by it and could hurt no one.

He began the long journey back to the opening where he had tumbled in a dreamlike state. He rose again to the world above. Cistoo lay silent, breathing cool, regular breaths.

Now I can rest. The thought allowed the shaman to give in to the sudden onslaught of fatigue. He slept all night.

"I'm hungry, Mama." The little girl's voice was weak and thin.

The words woke Letodah. He felt pure joy as he rolled over to check on the child. He looked forward to watching her mother wake up to find her child so improved. He wanted to share this great bliss and gratitude with her. Yet, when Letodah looked over at Nannuht, he was surprised to see her sitting in the same slumped position she had assumed the previous night. He knew she was exhausted, as he was, from all the care that she had given her only child. He leaned forward and nudged her gently on the arm. It was a soft nudge, yet her position was unsteady. She fell over onto the ground.

When Letodah came closer to help her up, he grabbed her arm. "Wake up, Nannuht. Cistoo is asking for food." Then he saw a vision he had encountered many times with Indians who were gravely ill. His heart sank deep into his chest. While Nannuht's body stayed in the same spot, an identical, transparent version of her lifted up, moving slowly toward Galun Lati, the sky vault.

Letodah still held onto her arm. Her mouth did not move, but she spoke words to him, thanking him, a message from her spirit to his. *Wadan, Wadan, Wadan.* She imparted the essence of great gratitude to him for saving her daughter. She also imparted a great sense of peace. If she died and her daughter lived, then so be it.

If the choice had been given to Nannuht to make, Letodah thought, *this is the end she would have chosen. Maybe the choice was offered to her. Maybe she took the worst of the illness into her own body in order to save her daughter.*

When her spirit hand reached out to Letodah, he took it. Their two, translucent spirits lifted into the Galun Lati. Looking briefly at the ground beneath where they had sat a moment earlier, Letodah could see their physical selves still seated in the same positions. Letodah saw himself, eyes shut, sitting cross-legged next to Cistoo. His limbs appeared long and awkward to him. Nannuht's limp, spent body slumped over onto the ground next to the fire.

You don't have to go the whole journey with me, Letodah. Just far enough so that you will know that I am all right, and you can share the news with Euchella and Cistoo. They must know that I would stay with them if I could. The words were transmitted telepathically and instantly without a need for language.

Letodah held her hand as they rose toward the sky. A cloud parted in two, separated by the brightest, whitest light Letodah had ever seen. As bright as the light was, he didn't need to look away. In a second, they entered the light. Immediately Letodah felt the overpowering presence of love and peace. Before, when escorting recently dead people, this was as far as he had come. He had never moved beyond the light.

It is as if, within this pure light, love and peace are concentrated into a single being.

Letodah knew that later, when he returned to the earth plane, he would call this being "the Great Spirit." The Great Spirit was all he had imagined it to be in his lifetime, but indescribably more. Yet he had the sense that this presence was neither male nor female, which surprised him. *I always thought the Great Spirit would be a fierce male warrior, protecting and feeding all the Indian tribes forever.* Now, in this ethereal space, Letodah had no sense of masculinity or femininity emanating from this presence, only goodness, love, and graciousness. Letodah felt his heart opening. Suddenly he realized that Nannuht was to review her life from birth to parting.

A panoramic view of each important event in her life passed before Nannuht's eyes. Everything she had ever done, good and bad, passed before her. She conveyed this odd experience to Letodah through her mind. *I feel the same way I felt when these events first happened. I can feel the way everyone else felt too, because of what I had done to them. If I hurt someone, I feel their hurt. If I was kind to someone, I can feel their warmth coming back to me.*

The miracle was that Letodah saw no shame on her face. From her telepathy to him, he learned that she could not condemn herself. Even when Nannuht experienced the great pain she had caused another, there was no reason for remorse. The Great Spirit permeated her whole being, forgiving her. Letodah had never witnessed such joy. He knew that now Nannuht loved herself as much as the Great Spirit loved her. She forgave herself of all wrongdoing.

Next the sky and its profound white light opened further. The time had come for Nannuht to move on. Letodah saw the arms of her welcoming ancestors beckon her forward toward the all-consuming light. He knew that he must return to the earth plane. No sooner had the words *earth plane* entered his thoughts than he found himself plummeting back into his physical body. He reentered his body with a thud.

Gone for a mere instant, he had just heard Cistoo say, "I'm hungry." She rubbed her eyes and tried to sit up.

The whole village would awaken soon. Before preparing the first meal of the day, the women would come out of their huts to stoke the fires. Ten men had gone into the woods for five days to hunt for deer and rabbits. They would return soon with the fresh meat. The women's work would be great until all of the fur stripping and meat preparation was complete. A portion of the meat would be hung, slowly smoked, and dried to last through the winter months, still a full season away.

Cistoo's father, Euchella, rode home from the hunt with his band of brothers. Before his departure, his little daughter had been struck with the high fever and severe chills.

Surely an evil spirit has captured her, he had thought. Just how gravely ill she had become since his departure, he had yet to learn.

He and his brothers had reason to be pleased with the hunt. They had killed six deer with their arrows and a few dozen rabbits. This would feed the tribe for a few weeks. Euchella had trapped one of the deer on the side of a small cliff before shooting him with his arrow.

Proudly he spoke to the gods about this gift. "I thank the deer who gave its life so that my family can eat." If Euchella were ungrateful, the deer's unappreciated spirit could revisit his relatives with a bone ailment.

Euchella had honored Nannuht in bringing home this kill. She would be able to sew a beautiful buckskin dress for herself. It would be her honor, because her husband had brought home the kill. The brothers would bring the fresh meat into camp and strip the hides for tanning.

As they neared the village, Euchella looked forward to sharing this news with his wife. *I hope that my little daughter is well so that Nannuht can listen to my hunting story without interruption.*

Euchella thought of his family with pride. Together he and Nannuht made a striking couple. They both had exceptionally handsome features. Euchella had a confidence about him that was magnetic. Nannuht was a good friend to many women in the village. She was the person they went to when they needed advice.

As the band grew close to camp, Euchella spied the dark smoke rising from the early morning fires. The women, *Anigeyv*, were awake, preparing the morning meal. *Probably catfish,* he thought. *My favorite.* A small crowd gathered around the opening of Euchella's hut. *I hope nothing has happened to Cistoo. She has the spirit of a warrior, even when her sick body tries to break her.*

Inside the hut, Euchella saw his small daughter sitting up while Nannuht's sister braided her hair. *Why is her aunt doing that? Why isn't my wife doing that?* he wondered. The medicine man walked toward Euchella. Fear settled over Euchella like a mantle.

"Your wife has gone to be with the Great One," Letodah said. "The sickness that almost took the child took her. Nannuht never stopped caring for Cistoo. She was her only thought. She died honorably doing her duties as a mother until the end. I brought back only enough medicine for Cistoo. I did not know that your woman was sick until it was too late to save her. She was already gone."

In that moment the details of Euchella's life, all of which had fit together in a neat puzzle, broke apart, vanishing like vapor into the air. He was a warrior, a tribesman, a husband, but no more. And all the reasons for putting on those roles had suddenly disappeared, along with those parts of him. *Who am I now?* he thought. *Why am I here when Nannuht is gone?*

Letodah rarely felt helpless, but in this case he did. He watched Euchella stare at his young daughter. He did not seem to recognize her. Letodah thought he didn't seem to see her anymore, or else she seemed like a stranger to him.

Euchella said nothing but walked away, back up the hill he had recently descended. He was staggering as if in a fog, like the haze on the mountain that had enveloped the hunters when they had first climbed up it.

He hiked for hours before he came to the top again. The landscape spread out for miles around him. Then a voice—a loud, jarring scream—filled the air. *Where did it come from?* Euchella wondered.

Across the miles, Letodah recognized the sound of Euchella's wailing.

Euchella camped on the chilly mountain all night. In the morning, he returned to the campsite to be present for the burial rites. He would dig a burial pit for his wife so that he could be certain that her body faced north. He must do this correctly. He would show the proper respect for his wife. If the corpse was buried improperly, the spirit world would bring disease to the whole village.

The whole tribe would be present for the burial, as they were when any tribal member passed on. As shaman, Letodah would lead the ceremony. Euchella had been quiet since returning to the campsite. The joy evident on his face the day before had left him. The joy of the fresh hunt and the anticipation of giving the news to his wife were gone. He could no longer study his wife's features as she prepared the pelts or stoked the fire.

The day of the funeral dawned bright and sunny. No clouds marred the perfect sky. Letodah said, "This day mirrors the bright openness of the sky to receive this brave woman's spirit. Euchella did his duty; his wife's body faces north in the ground."

The ground had been dry and hard, difficult to dig. The men dug the hole deep. They wanted to keep her scent away from wild dogs that sniffed near the camp, foraging for food.

Letodah noticed the stunning and abrupt change in the way Euchella behaved toward his daughter. The love and pride with which he had treated her one week earlier was gone. His emotions had been replaced with what at first had been a vague anger, then a stronger anger. Within the short span of a few hours, Letodah saw Euchella's anger turn into a glowing, steady rage.

Euchella explained it to Letodah, "This girl made my wife sick with the disease that killed her. She has killed her own mother. No good can come from her. And now this disease has made her ugly. She no longer looks pretty like her mother. Her chin has small holes in it from the disease. She is marked by evil. It makes me sick to look at her."

Letodah tried to convince him that his feelings were temporary. "This is your sadness talking, Euchella. Give it a chance. You don't want to lose your only daughter too."

But Euchella cut Cistoo completely out of his life. He instructed his family to reject her. By tribal custom, shunning was the worst penalty one member could inflict on another. "I never want to look at her again. Have nothing to do with her. She has the mark of evil on her." He spat on the ground at her feet and declared she was no longer his. "Because of her, I will never have a son with Nannuht."

Euchella became a different tribesman than he had been before his wife's death. Before she died, life and fire filled everything he did. After her passing, he did his duty, but he drifted through it. His actions conveyed little energy. The fire in his heart dwindled to barely lighted embers. Most of the time the fire seemed extinguished. The only small, burning spot still was his sense of pride in being a tribesman and in supporting his comrades. Only duty to his comrades and his wish to avoid shame kept him going. But even duty did not propel him long; the pain was too great. Very soon, he turned to firewater as his sole comfort.

Cistoo's aunties, Nannuht's sisters, had no intention of shunning the little girl. They could only stand by sadly and watch as she ran up to Euchella, her arms lifted in the air, calling, "Pick me up, Daddy. Swing me around, Daddy." She looked so happy to see her father. But, whenever she approached him, he turned sharply in his tracks. The child grew so frustrated she broke into loud sobs.

Repeatedly, Cistoo called, "*Adadoda*, Daddy." Then she began to cry for her mother.

"Your mother has gone to the Great Spirit, dear one," her aunts would say. Huddling around her, the aunties drew her near them to comfort her. But the idea of the Great Spirit taking her mother was beyond the child's understanding.

In the days after Nannuht's burial, the aunties had expected Euchella to come around. They had spoken to Letodah about it. "We think once he gets over the shock of Nannuht dying, he will start to miss Cistoo."

"I do not think he will ever get over this. I'm sorry to tell you this, but it is what I foresee," Letodah answered.

Letodah was right. Nothing changed. If anything, Euchella grew more hardened toward Cistoo. The little girl was dead to him—more like a ghost than real. He did not speak of her to anyone, even the aunties. So at the tender age of six, Cistoo had to deal with the death of both of her parents. The death of her mother's body and the death of her father's love.

I can see you, Daddy. Why don't you talk to me? This one thought occupied her young mind. She could see him walking around and talking, yet he was not talking to her. He was not seeing her. She was invisible to him. She felt a giant chasm grow within her. She felt hungry for some sort of spiritual food she was no longer being fed.

When she wanted to talk to someone, she visited her mother's grave. She made a daily habit of it. In the six months since Nannuht had died, Cistoo had only missed days when it rained hard or snowed.

"Mother, help me, please. I've got to fill this hole inside of me."

After her visit to the gravesite, Cistoo liked to wander through the woods for hours. Since she had no playmates, she enjoyed looking for the *Nunnehi*. These troll-like creatures could be most easily detected in thunderclaps. They could be quite useful in leading an Indian to a lost object, such as a horse or a dog. Cistoo also knew that calling on them could aid in an ill person's recovery.

But the Nunnehi were sometimes spiteful. Small in stature like tiny children, they enjoyed playing tricks on others. They took great glee in causing frustration and consternation. Recently, when Cistoo had wandered a little way from the center of the village, she passed under a series of oak trees and a barrage of acorns hit her on the head. At first, she thought squirrels had thrown them. But when she looked above into the tree, no squirrels were there.

"Must be those mischievous Nunnehi trying to make me believe the squirrels are attacking me. Maybe they want to be fed."

That evening she had laid out beans and cornstalks filled with corn, just in case those meddlesome spirits were, in fact, hungry. The next morning, she went to the site where she had left the food to find out if they had eaten her offerings.

To be sure, the food was all gone. "It must have been the Nunnehi." Cistoo smiled as she remembered that experience. "Maybe now they will be kind to me and not stir up any mischief for a while."

She was still thinking of the Nunnehi when, suddenly, a large blanket landed on her head and covered her body like a tent. People were tying the blanket tightly around her so she could not escape.

"Help! Help!" She screamed until her lungs hurt.

Four children, three boys and one girl, had followed her out on the trail where she walked every day. "Please help me somebody. Mama! Daddy!"

"No one will hear you. You should just give up!" a boy hissed.

Another one of the boys put his mouth next to her ear and said, "You can't get out of the fix we're going to put you in."

"You are a pox on our tribe," the girl said, repeating what she had heard her parents say.

Through the woven blanket, Cistoo saw the faintly gray faces of the children carrying her. She recognized the voices from the times they had played together as children, before her mother had died.

Cousins, she thought.

She counted four heads. She smelled the strong, musty odor of bear jerky: the kind her uncle, the father of two of these bad children, ate. *My uncle is behind this.*

"My aunties will make you sorry you did this to me." Cistoo squirmed and kicked inside her blanket sack.

"Nunnehi, please come help me now!" she screamed, terrified.

The smallest boy spoke for the first time. "Why don't we throw her off a cliff and be done with her?"

"I think we should bury her in the ground and put honey on her head." Another one offered. "The wolves will eat her. They'll dig her out and leave nothing but bones behind."

Cistoo squirmed inside her blanket, trying to escape. They held onto her tight.

"We could drop her in that rattlesnake pit my father found when he was hunting. She'd be bitten to death in no time."

"Why don't you just leave me alone? Aren't you supposed to leave me alone?" Cistoo was both scared and angry now.

"Shut up. We're not talking to you, evil one. We are here to see you get paid back for killing your mother."

"I didn't kill my mother."

"We could throw stones at her until she's so beat up she dies."

Cistoo's protests were ignored.

"I don't really care which one we choose, as long as at the end of it, she's dead," the girl said, matter-of-factly.

Cistoo had never been more afraid.

Stay strong, my daughter, there is no place they can take you that I cannot go.

She heard her mother's voice talking inside her head, as she often did in times of need. "Don't do this. Don't hurt me. You will be in big trouble if you hurt me."

The tallest of the children laughed. "Are you kidding? No one will ever miss you."

Cistoo kicked and thrashed and hollered.

"You can kick and scream all you want; no one will hear you from way out here."

Dimly, she could see movement through the empty spaces between the blanket's threads. *These children belong to my father's brother and sister.*

The children laughed, congratulating each other's good fortune. "This has gone easier than we planned. She is getting heavy, though."

One of the boys slapped another on the back. "We did a great job sneaking up on her. We were so quiet she didn't hear us coming. We had the blanket over her before she knew what was happening." He laughed in appreciation of his own success.

"My father said Letodah healed the wrong person."

At last, they stopped and propped her against a pine tree. They tied extra sturdy knots to secure her tightly. Her feet barely touched the ground.

"She will not be able to wriggle out of this one," one of her captors boasted. "Even if she could untie herself, we have scared her too bad for her ever to come back to our village." They were already talking about her as if she had disappeared.

Cistoo heard their voices fade as the children walked away. "Don't leave me. Don't leave me here. Come back. I'm not bad."

"She will die from starvation or really bad weather," the girl said. "She's too little to know how to take care of herself out here."

"Why are you doing this to me? I didn't do anything bad."

Cistoo cried so long and hard that she exhausted herself. She fell asleep leaning against the hard trunk of the pine tree.

She woke up with a start when she heard a rattling sound. Barely a crack of light shone between the cloth and the ground, the rope had been pulled so tightly to secure her. But she could see her foot. She heard the sound again. It was the sound of a nearby rattlesnake. Before she could gasp, the snake slithered across her foot. She knew her only chance to avoid being bitten was to stay perfectly still. *Don't move,* she told herself.

Cistoo was scared. When she was so sick, she had been too delirious to be scared. She held her breath. The snake circled the base of the tree twice, each time sliding over her foot. Each time the reptile crossed over her foot's arch. *If I pull my foot back, it will bite me. I would die in a little while. There is no one around to help me.* After what seemed like a very long time, the rattling sound stopped. Cistoo no longer felt the snake travel over her foot.

Her stomach rumbled. She was very hungry. She had eaten nothing for over a day. More even than hunger, her stomach felt hollow; it ached for lack of food. She was also thirsty. She had taken a drink from a small stream shortly before the children captured her. Now her throat felt dry. She coughed again and again, but she could not make the dryness go away.

I am so dirty, she thought. *I stink.* Cistoo had soiled herself when the blanket first flew over her head. Whenever she had to pee, her only choice was to let it run down her leg.

Frequently she dozed off. Whenever she slept, her body slumped against the ropes. Her arms and chest spasmed in pain. It was her legs, though, that hurt the most. Every time she fell asleep, her legs pushed off the ground to keep her from falling. It was an automatic response. Her legs pained her so much that she could only grind her teeth and cry out, "Aaaaahhhhiii."

My aunties are looking for me. They will be here soon.

She slept off and on the entire second day. Late in the afternoon, she heard the thunder. It started to rain. The lightning flashed across the sky in front of her eyes. Lightning normally frightened her. But now, at least, she could lift her head up to catch rainwater in her mouth as it soaked through the blanket.

As she was drinking, she felt a tug at the rope that wrapped her.

"Don't worry, Cistoo. In a moment, you will be free," Letodah reassured her. Within seconds, he had released her from her trap. "I'll carry you back to the village."

Letodah wrapped her in a dry blanket he took from his horse's back. He pulled her up to sit in front of him. "We're going home. You will be safe there."

With her head and arms resting on the horse's mane and neck, Cistoo slept most of the trip back.

Returning to camp was much quicker on horseback. Letodah had given her a piece of jerky to soften her hunger.

He thanked the Great Spirit for keeping her alive. "May the Great Spirit watch over this girl all of the time. Let no evil visit her. Protect her from all those who would harm her."

The aunties cried for joy when they saw their niece, which woke Cistoo up. She loved being swamped with their hugs and kisses as they lowered her from the horse. Both she and Letodah had gotten drenched in the rain.

"Come inside, Letodah, and warm yourself by our fire. Thank you for bringing her back to us. This makes the second time you have saved her. "

They changed Cistoo's clothes and wrapped her in a dry, clean blanket.

She told them all about the cousin captors and the rattlesnake. "Why do they want to hurt me?"

"No good reason, just meanness. We will visit your cousins' parents tomorrow. They will never lay their hands on you again; we promise." The aunties wagged their fingers in the air, and furrowed their brows.

Letodah said, "I will sleep next to the opening of your hut tonight in case the news reaches them that Cistoo is back. I will protect you."

After she had eaten, Cistoo slept deeply that night, surrounded by her doting aunties. She knew that Letodah was looking out for her.

Letodah continued to pray most of the night. "Please do not allow Cistoo's soul to be injured by this cruelty done to her. Help her to continue to grow in strength and trust."

Letodah followed his prayer with a visit to the Underworld, where he retrieved a portion of her soul that had been lost during the cruel attacks.

When the cousins had arrived back home from tying Cistoo to the tree, they had smiles on their faces. Proudly, they went straight to their parents to tell them what they had done to Cistoo. Euchella's brother rose first and knocked his son to the ground with the back of his hand.

"This was not for you children to do. We grown ones have other plans for that girl."

Two of Euchella's other brothers learned from the children where they had taken Cistoo and set out to find her. The adults used their best tracking skills, but their children had given poor directions. The boys and girl had selected a random spot and hadn't bothered to remember where they had left her. They had simply walked aimlessly before finally deciding to stop and tie her up.

Among themselves, the adults decided it was not important if they located her. "Even if we don't find her, it doesn't matter. She got what she deserved. Now we don't have to carry out our scheme."

But when they learned of Cistoo's rescue, Euchella's relatives left the tribe suddenly in the middle of the night. They knew that Letodah, the chief, and others in the tribe would punish them harshly if they did not. No one knew where they went.

Even after the cousins had trapped her, Cistoo continued to visit her mother. But now she ran behind Letodah when he took his daily run. Cistoo visited Nannuht's grave on the trip back to the village after the run. That way, both she and Letodah could work on staying strong. And Letodah could keep an eye on her.

Cistoo made a vow to herself: "No one will ever treat me like that again. Next time I will be too strong. I will be ready for them."

Chapter 2

Cistoo Joins the Boys

"She has the energy of a dozen boys," her aunties bragged. "She is strong like her mother was at her age."

Yet, much to her aunties' dismay, Cistoo preferred the boys' games. But the adult warriors did not want to teach her the lessons that they taught the boys. Even the littlest boys began their training in the games soon after they learned to walk. Some boys were trained to be hunters, while others were trained to be warriors. Some lucky boys were trained by both their fathers and their uncles. Cistoo had neither of these relatives to teach her.

Cistoo was taught by her aunties. They did everything in harmony with each other. Their chunky bodies seemed to move in unison. They were three of the four daughters born to Cistoo's grandparents—all just nine hands high and generally cheerful. They loved Cistoo, but she annoyed them. Still, they wanted to do justice to Nannuht's memory.

They were distressed when they found Cistoo shooting arrows at a tree in the forest when she should have been at the hut helping them. "What's wrong with you? You were supposed to be back hours ago. Why do you disappoint us over and over again?"

Whenever the aunties wanted to instruct her in women's work, they had to find her first and drag her home. When they did get her back, she practiced her throwing skills inside the hut. She liked to hurl her knife at a log she had put near the wall. Once she nicked the leg of one of her aunts.

"Stop it, Cistoo!" the aunt said. "Act like a girl. You could have killed me." She cleaned her wound and pulled Cistoo by the elbow back over to the cooking pots. This oldest and heaviest of the aunties complained the most.

Every day the aunties repeated, "Do your duty. You do not accept who you are. What do you think your mother would say if she saw you being so contrary?"

Repeatedly they scolded her. "You need to behave so you can make your mother proud. You need to be who your mother would want you to be."

"I know better than you do what kind of woman my mother wants me to be," Cistoo replied rebelliously. "My mother wants me to be happy. My mother wants me to use my skills!"

The aunties spent much of their time exasperated.

Cistoo continued to spend hours daily sitting by her mother's grave. The sense of her mother's presence reassured her.

At times, she heard her mother answer her. "I am proud of you, Cistoo. Be the girl you want to be. I will always be proud of you." Still, the aunties' complaints bothered her.

If she could come back, Cistoo thought, *Mama would spoil me. She would love me and teach me and dote on me—and not complain about me. Mama would never be ashamed of me.* Though the features of her mother's face were fading from her memory, she could remember how warm and secure her mother had made her feel.

Why don't my aunties understand? I need to be strong to protect myself.

Being strong would also be a way to impress her father. Her mother was gone; but Euchella was alive. He could be a real part of her life if he would stop being so stubborn and come back, she thought. *He did not mean for the cousins to hurt me. He only meant for them to shun me.*

The problem was that while Cistoo could see her father, she needed to make him see her. *Maybe he would not ignore me if I were a boy. Once I learn every bit of what the men can do, Daddy will want to claim me.*

Soon, she imagined, *he will take me on a hunt with him and teach me how to ride and shoot the bow. Soon he will be as proud of me as if I were his son.*

She prayed to her mother in the Galun Lati, where she lived. *I miss you, Mama. I want to be a good squaw. Please forgive me, Mama, if you need to.*

She prayed the night before she decided to break into the boys' games, "Great Spirit, please bring my father back to me. Please fill me with skill and strength. Make me the best hunter and warrior in the tribe."

Cisco watched the boys intently for an hour before mustering the nerve to join them. They warmed up for a practice game by throwing stones at a chestnut tree. If a brave threw a stone that hit the tree and landed close to another stone nearby, that was fine. The goal was to see who could get the most stones the closest to the tree. A stone landing and leaning against the tree trunk also scored.

Invisible to the boys, Cistoo watched the game from a safe distance in the forest. One difficulty she observed was in landing the stone near the tree without bouncing it off the tree's surface. *It might be easier to land the stone near the tree. Bouncing it off the tree could be tricky. Depending on the angle that the rock hits the trunk, it could shoot out wide and land far from the trunk. That would be a bad shot.*

To make the game fair, the braves had set up a line of sticks so that everyone threw from the same distance. If a brave was young or small, he was given a slight advantage: being permitted to stand closer to the tree. Cisco watched the boys for weeks, and she practiced privately. *When I do join the practice, I've got to be good enough to win. Only winning will make them take me serious.* She knew that the actual game they played was harder and more challenging than the practice. She must be ready.

And the day came when she felt ready. Cistoo stepped out of hiding and walked with the confidence of a chief to where the boys were playing.

The tallest boy said, "Why aren't you with your aunties, making our supper?"

Melauki pointed forcefully with his hand toward camp. "Go back to camp. We will be hungry after this game." He wanted to shove her out of his space, but he knew he could not. The tribe forbade roughness with a female. Hitting women was against the rules.

"I know how to do this," Cistoo stood her ground firmly. "I want to play." She looked brave, but her heart beat wildly in her chest.

The boys glanced around at each other before bursting into laughter. "You must be *Ulvnotisgi.*"

"I am *not* crazy. I throw better than any of you." Cistoo frowned, deeply furrowing her eyebrows.

The boys circled around her, chanting, "*Ulvnotisgi Ageyutsa, Ulvnotisgi Ageyutsa* (Crazy girl)." They took turns jumping at her, growling like bears and showing their teeth.

One boy sprang behind Cistoo and pulled a pigtail. They tormented her in this fashion for what seemed like forever. *I will show them who's crazy,* she thought. She flailed her arms wildly around her head, spitting and yelling with a high-pitched, eerie sound.

"*Arrrgeraaaaah!*" She cut right through them, running hard and fast into the nearby woods.

"That girl is *Ulvnotisgi.*" The boys shook their heads. "Totally crazy."

Cistoo ran about twenty-five yards into the woods before looking behind her. She could not be sure at first if someone was chasing her. Breathing hard, she turned around; she could not see the braves anymore, but she could hear them laughing in the distance. She knew they were laughing at her. Then the hurt and fear she had felt moments earlier grew into a bounding sense of fury.

She reeled around and marched back to the clearing with stubborn determination. The boys had already resumed their game. Picking up a rock at the edge of the woods, she waited for the right moment to come up silently behind them. Melauki had gotten off a spectacular shot—with the rock standing upright against the base of the tree. Since he had taken the last turn, no one could beat him. Yet he would only bask in the glory of his win for a second. A rock whizzed past his head, hitting his rock and sending it soaring six feet beyond the tree.

The boys stood dazed, staring at the tree in disbelief. They thought each of their brothers had already had a turn. Melauki was the first to turn around. He couldn't believe his eyes; Cistoo stood barely a yard out of the woods.

It can't be true, he thought.

Cistoo stood frozen with a broad smile on her face. She leaned forward, slapping her thighs and laughing heartily. "I told you I throw the best!"

When she saw the boys whirl around and glare at her, she stood upright. "I win," she proclaimed gleefully. Then she twirled about, ran rapidly back through the woods, and returned to her safe encampment. Although the boys chased her, they did not catch her. Besides being a better pitcher, she also ran faster than any of them.

Once they were all back in the camp, the braves knew they couldn't touch her. They knew better than to do anything hurtful toward her in front of the aunties. They were too embarrassed to admit to the elders that this Ulvnotisgi Ageyutsa had beaten them.

After weeks of frustration, with Cistoo repeatedly beating them at their own games, the boys relented. They did not like her sneering at them. The group decided, "If we let her join in our practice we can learn the tricks she uses to beat us. We can watch her sneakiness up close."

At first, there was no possibility in their minds that Cistoo had earned her wins honestly—that she had a stronger arm and a surer eye than any of them. After all, she was small for a girl her age and certainly smaller and weaker than many of them. She seemed fragile. The elders blamed it on that fever that had almost taken her from the earth a few years earlier. Still, she had a ferocity about her face. Even as a child, her extra-black eyes pierced through others like an arrow.

Cistoo's team traveled annually to the nearest Choctaw tribe to compete against them. Yet Letodah had never allowed her to play in a real game. He served as the coach, and he simply wouldn't allow it. It was too big a risk. *She could be cast out of the tribe for good,* Letodah thought, *even though Euchella's relatives are gone. Who knows where they might show up? She is not popular with the rest of the tribe either.*

But Cistoo prepared for the big game every day. Besides the usual practice with the boys, she got up early, and ran long distances with Letodah before dawn. Daily she lifted heavy rocks to increase her strength. She had adopted the braves' practice of eating only two meals per day. This diet helped her to develop discipline and to stay fit. However, the aunties were often surprised by how much food she could consume at each meal. No male child ate more. Typically, she ate a large portion of meat, when it was available, along with three heaping bowls of corn mush. By the time Cistoo was twelve, she had grown a foot in height, taller than most of the boys.

"By all that is sacred, you are going to blow up from stuffing all that food down your throat," the aunties said.

The tools of the game were simple: a leather ball and a catcher. Often the boys crafted the catchers for themselves. Sometimes they were given one as a special gift by their fathers or favorite uncles. Each brave would decorate his catcher to identify it as his own. He would burn personal symbols on the sticks or paint designs on the handle with colors made from dyes the shaman concocted.

At other times, a feather was woven into the stringed mitt for luck. The shaman would sing a victory chant over the catchers to give these game tools superpowers to catch and to throw the ball. Cistoo crafted a catcher for herself with blue jay feathers she had gathered on her morning runs.

At last, the day of the big game arrived. Their Choctaw rival had to walk five days from their camp. The game was a tribal affair, actually. Every man, woman, and child walked the distance to the field where the game took place. The mothers dressed their children in their finest clothes. They had gone to the river the day before to clean themselves before the long trek.

It was exciting; it carried people away from their daily routines. Everyone's spirit lifted, old and young alike, with having time away from the village for a few days. The adults enjoyed walking along the glassy-smooth French Broad River. They delighted the children by pointing out fish and turtles swimming in it.

All the braves who were playing walked in front. Cistoo walked with her aunties. While the whole tribe looked forward to the game throughout the year, no one anticipated it more than Cistoo. *Maybe this year Letodah will let me play.*

Since both teams had to travel to arrive at the field, they were allowed to rest and camp for the night. The actual game would begin the next morning. But camping for the night was the opposite of resting.

Letodah performed a ritual, saying, "Keep away all evil spirits that would slow us down and make us weak. Give us strength, Spirit of the Wind, to run fast and make many goals. Help us to make friends with any evil spirits that might impede their strength and skill so that they would not stumble. Help us keep our heads high, looking at the victory that must be ours." He lit a large bonfire. Dancing most of the night, the braves pumped themselves up into a frenzy.

On the day of the game, the team rose shortly before first sunlight to eat a big meal. They would eat again only after the game was over. The game could last a few hours or all day long, anywhere from midmorning until sunset. Spirits ran high on both teams. Training all year for one shot at winning made the stakes high.

Letodah raked sharp-toothed combs over the players' backs, arms, faces, and chests until they bled. He treated Cistoo as if she were a true team player even though he had no intention of allowing her to play in a real game. She rubbed her cuts hard to make them bleed more.

The Cherokee were clean people normally but especially during times when a purification ceremony would add to their good fortune. Cistoo and the braves bathed in the stream near the camp. Afterward they dried off and applied red paint to their bodies for blood and striped black lines to their faces to show ferocity.

After painting their bodies, the team gathered in a circle for a prayer and blessing led by Letodah. "Great Spirit, be with us today. We are the most worthy. We have worked hard and sacrificed to please you. We ask you to take our side today to show the Choctaw our superior strength."

"Win we will. Win we will. We will crush them. We will crush them"—the team chanted their victory song, driving up their energy to its peak. They needed to convince themselves that they were fearless and undefeatable.

Fifteen players from each side crowded the field. The wooden goal faced north. The teams faced each other east to west. Neither team had an unfair advantage in relation to the only target. To put the leather ball into play, a player from Cistoo's team would turn his back to the field and throw it with the catcher over his head into the middle of the players. Cistoo's team went first, because they had traveled the farthest to the field.

"*Alenvdi,*" screamed the crowd, eager for the long-awaited game to begin.

Cistoo watched as the members of her team, the red team, scooped the ball up first, but the elbow of a player from the other team hit his head. Blood ran down his face as he stumbled, dizzy from the injury. He threw the ball to another brave on his team, who snagged it easily and began to run down the field toward the goal.

Cistoo turned to Letodah and said, "He should have been guarding against that side."

A red team member ran hard behind him and tackled him, pushing his face into the dirt. So it went back and forth, with extremely rough play for the first hour of the game, with neither team scoring.

Cistoo talked to Letodah throughout the game. "Look at that red player in the back. He is just standing there, doing nothing. I could do better than that."

"That Indian missed catching the ball. Such an easy catch. He's losing the game for us."

"How could you send him to play instead of me? I run much faster."

After six hours, the score was ten to eight in favor of the red team, with only an hour of sunlight remaining. Cistoo relentlessly begged Letodah to let her play.

His response was always the same. "It is not a good time. It is too dangerous for you. I don't want you to be ridiculed."

"But how would the Choctaw even know I am a girl? I am taller than many of them. My breasts are just starting to grow. The flap I wear in front covers my womanhood. They would not know. Give me a chance. You know how hard I've worked. Let me show what I can do."

Cistoo could see that Letodah felt torn; she knew he wanted to give her a chance. So when a team player came close to the sideline and Letodah pulled him off the field, Cistoo was both surprised and delighted. Quickly the shaman pushed Cistoo out into the game, giving the other players no time to object.

Pure adrenalin coursed through Cistoo's body. She had waited for this moment for half of her life. Although drunk and inattentive, her father was in the crowd. She was willing to risk banishment for this chance to impress him.

The ball was in play for the yellows when she ran onto the field. She tried to blend in as inconspicuously as possible. Her team had a two-point advantage. That would be hard for the yellows to overcome, but she did not want to take the lead for granted. She worked her way across the field to be nearer the action.

The yellow team had successfully launched a pass in the direction of a player within feet of the goal. She positioned herself in front of the goal. She stood ready to deflect any attempt the other team made at scoring. She lifted both arms and waved them, but the arm of the yellow team player was strong. He hurled the ball past her and through the goal. Their lead had shrunk to one.

Her teammate put the ball in his thrower and shot it down the field to Melauki. The yellows knew that he was the red team's best player. They surrounded him, making it hard for him to take a shot.

He kept running and zigzagging, trying to break free of their block. Then he saw Cistoo free in the corner. He was reluctant to pass to her, but he thought, *She is an unknown player to them, having just come into the game.* He feigned a shot toward a brave directly in front of him, and then, just as suddenly, whirled around forcefully hurling the ball in Cistoo's direction. She wasn't expecting it. But she was alert. She had followed the play closely and took advantage of this opportunity. With the ball moving rapidly toward her, she threw her body hard to the right, barely catching it before falling to the ground.

Almost as quickly as she hit the ground, she bounced up and started to run. Melauki had calculated correctly. No one was watching her.

This is my chance, Cistoo thought. Surprising the yellow team's braves, she took off running toward the goal. They trailed several yards after her, running as hard as they could. She arrived at the goal with a clear shot at it. She threw, and the reds were up again by two points. Now they were just one point from the winning number of twelve goals.

Cistoo figured that Melauki would have rather made the goal himself. *Too bad for him,* she thought. *He cannot win this game all by himself. Even if he thinks he can.*

A yellow team member put the ball back into play with a long and successful pass down the field. The boy with the ball ran nimbly toward the goal before being tackled by a red team member. The ball rolled out of his catcher, freely available on the ground for any alert player to scoop it up.

A red team player did just that, then flipped it to Melauki. Melauki was on the run but again found himself surrounded by yellow players. He was about to be tackled when he looked around for Cistoo. Cistoo ran past the bunch surrounding Melauki, allowing him to toss the ball past them into her net. By then the other team had wised up; several players were cutting her off. Some ran from guarding Melauki to defend against Cistoo. Still she was the fastest runner on the field. They found it hard to keep up with her. Again she approached the goal.

Suddenly, she saw two opportunities. *I could flick the ball around that yellow player and have a good chance of scoring, or I could flip it back to Melauki. He does have a slightly better shot at the goal.* She flipped the ball to him, and he flipped it in. The red team howled and yelped and danced to celebrate the win.

Heads hanging, the yellow team walked off the field. They had brought shame to their tribe. An entire year would pass before a chance to prove themselves would come again. They gathered their belongings but couldn't leave before making a few parting remarks to the winners.

"Your team was lucky this year. Next year we will destroy you."

"You better start practicing now."

"We should have won. Our best players got hurt and couldn't play."

Melauki stuck his face into the face of a yellow player. "Excuses! You know why we beat you? We played better."

A fight nearly erupted, but Letodah pushed his players away from the yellow team toward the path to the village.

Cistoo looked to the sidelines where her father had sat during most of the game. Though he had watched with seeming disinterest, at least he was there. She looked over to see if he had witnessed her fine performance, but he had disappeared.

I'll find him and tell him about my great plays. I helped win the game. He will have to be happy with me. When she found him, he was huddled near a fire in the temporary camp, twisting his hands together and talking gibberish. He was drunk.

He probably didn't recognize me. But the part within her that took pride in her own accomplishments was growing stronger. *Today I will feel victorious. I will not let my father keep me from feeling good about this.* She would not allow her happiness to be clouded by Euchella's neglect of her.

Letodah felt great pride in how Cistoo had handled the last-minute choice in the game. *She put herself aside to give Melauki the shot. She put the team ahead of herself.*

Every week he learned something new about Cistoo. The seed of an idea that he had at first dismissed was now beginning to flourish. He wanted to be a big part of Cistoo's future. *As the tribe's shaman, don't I know better than anyone how Cistoo can best serve our tribe? She has great gifts,* Letodah acknowledged to himself. *I know how we can make great use of her.*

Chapter 3

Celebrations

The night after they arrived back in the village, the tribe held its victory dance. The chief took the first turn. He stamped his feet heavily on the ground and then more lightly as his movements gradually increased. For the Cherokee, little relationship existed between rhythm and dancing. The dancers followed their inner urgings for movement rather than any external instrument like a drum.

The chief took his place in front of the large fire, stomping slowly as the drummer drummed to his own beat. The chief recited the recent history of the game in a monotone: "Our young braves played strong against the weak Choctaw. They stole the ball whenever they could. They ran swiftly down the field like our brother, the deer. They fought and hit hard, making the other team bleed. We won this game with better strategy and skill. Our braves rescued the day. Now we celebrate and dance and eat food, having saved the face of the whole community. There is only pride tonight. No shame has been brought to our tribe or to our people. Our team has done their duty and played well."

The chief repeated the story of the game throughout the night, adding more detail each time about a particular play he had admired.

Cistoo felt proud when he mentioned her pass to Melauki to win the game. Luckily, the chief had not realized that it was she who had made the pass, though she disliked being invisible. But at least Letodah knew what she had done. Melauki and the team knew too. For now, she would be satisfied with that small piece of recognition.

The air filled with the smell of roasted deer and root vegetables. The carrots had a particularly pungent and delightful aroma. Children ran around tagging each other, pretending to be hunting bear. In the morning, the women had cooked the squirrel and acorn stew that was the staple of the day. Cornstalks and bean wraps were in abundant supply.

Everyone from child to chief donned his or her most elaborate and beautiful costumes, with feathers in headdresses and around belts. The women wore rattles made from the shells of small turtles. Attached by a small leather strap, tiny rocks clacked against the sides within each rattle. The women tied the turtle instruments to their legs. As they stomped, the rocks shook inside the shells, making their own rhythm from the heavy steps of the dancers.

The tribe had stocked up on firewater left by visiting traders. The chief and the other men had started drinking well before the dance. The evening would be rowdy for sure. Cistoo knew that it would be a chance for her father to get as drunk as he wanted. *I wish he knew how stupid he looks!*

Cistoo watched the chief as he pranced and stomped along the ground. The next tribesman to join the dance followed directly after him.

"I have grown up in this tribe and seen many games, joined many hunts." The tribesman spoke. "Sometimes we have been defeated. Sometimes we have won, but my life has been good, thanks to the Great Spirit, even when my women have caused me trouble. I can't stay with any of them for long. My second wife drove me crazy, yelling at me all the time with her bad temper.

She said my lovemaking was worse than my hunting. She made me happy in the end, though, when she ran off with my friend. It was shameful, but she is ugly now. Time has been her enemy. I got a new wife pronto, who cooks good food. She gave me sons and one girl. Wife number one is not worth mentioning."

Before long, a train of dancers made a serpentine path in the clearing. One man, following the dancers weaving in and out, wore a white blanket around his head. He moved slowly and creakily as if very old. "I can't ride my horse anymore," he said. "My legs are stiff. I can barely walk without hobbling." He pretended to stumble and fall.

Laughing and hooting at his antics, tribespeople gathered around the performer. He impersonated running after a young woman and falling on his face. He limped along following an equally old squirrel, played with gusto by his youngest son. The squirrel eluded him too. Cistoo laughed until tears rolled down her cheeks.

One by one, men, women, and children joined the dance, following the lead of the chief. As the firewater was passed around, the impromptu songs got cruder and funnier. Even the children stayed up all night whooping and hollering, eating and dancing. They played games with each other, loving the wild freedom this celebration allowed them.

Unknown to Cistoo, a Choctaw tribal member was present who knew her well. He had grown up with her. He had watched her during the game and seen what a good player she was. He thought, *She has no right to play in this game. She has no right to celebrate any victory.*

The next day, life went on, even though there were many aching heads and sick stomachs from the firewater. As usual, the aunties worried that Cistoo's adulthood was doomed.

"She will be shamed. She will bring shame on us."

"We cannot stop this girl. Even though she cooks and sews in a passable way, she runs off with the boys every chance she gets."

"No one in the tribe will respect her. They could make her leave." That was their biggest fear. The chiefs and the tribal council could banish her to solitude in the forest.

They prayed to the Great Spirit. They talked endlessly among themselves. Then when Cistoo was about to turn thirteen, the answer came to them: "We will marry her off to one of the braves, if any will have her; she is such a boy herself."

Traditionally the tribe allowed a young woman to choose her husband. If she should tire of him later, she could set his possessions outside of their hut, signaling an official divorce. But at least she would have followed the normal route of a young Indian girl growing up in the tribe.

"I will do as you ask." Cistoo said, agreeing to her aunties' request for her to find a husband. But she said it only to get them off her back.

She had a secret. She already knew someone who would marry her. Behind that secret, though, was another secret that would make the marriage bearable.

"It will be like no marriage at all." She smiled inwardly at this knowledge. In fact, she would have more freedom when wed, because her groom was a total pushover. Meduck was her only friend. He had made her promise to keep his secret.

They had become friends in childhood and confided in each other. Meduck had told her, "I never want to lie down with a woman. I don't want to have children. I would rather live with a man. Do you hate me for saying that?"

"No. It's the way you are. I would rather be a boy myself."

Meduck was very skinny. His movements were delicate like flowers blowing in the breeze. When he spoke, he often had to repeat himself; his voice was so soft. He also had a slight lisp. Cistoo was the only person who didn't make him feel shy.

Cistoo had discovered that it was okay to be herself with Meduck.

"You can cook and sew, Meduck. I will be a brave. I will hunt and fish. You like to do what I don't like. I like to do what you don't like. This marriage could be perfect for both of us."

The aunties were oblivious to Cistoo's secret. They believed that it was their deerskin offerings to Meduck's family that had made them agree to the marriage. *Why else would any family want such an Ulvnotisgi girl?* The boy's family believed that they were the ones who had won the victory. They didn't know who else would want to marry their boy-girl either. As a husband, everyone knew that Meduck was the least desirable male in the whole village.

In the case of their beloved Cistoo, the aunties knew they were working with a serious handicap. *Even though she's tall with a scarred chin, she is still pretty good-looking.* Cistoo knew that her aunties were ecstatically happy with this prospective union.

Meduck's family gladly agreed to the pair marrying. As children, Meduck and Cistoo had liked to play warrior games together. Meduck always ended up dead in those games, but he didn't mind losing. His family hoped that Cistoo could teach him to act like a man.

To her aunties, she pretended to be forlorn about her looming marriage. "Why would you want me to marry?" she wailed. "My freedom will be gone. How will I ride on the hunt if I have children to take care of? I don't want children. I'm a hunter."

Cistoo welcomed this turn of events. Inside, she felt everything was working out well. *At least I will be allowed to stay with the tribe. I can follow some of my plans. At least I can be true to myself some of the time.*

Her marriage to Meduck was to take place a week after the big game, on her thirteenth birthday. Cistoo told herself that the game had been her last bit of glorious fun with the boys before she became an official wife.

Letodah questioned the wisdom of the marriage. *If I am to speak to the chief, I must do it soon. He must give permission for my idea to work. And I must talk to him before this wedding takes place. While*

I don't know what it is like to lie with a woman, I don't think Meduck is capable of it. But I can't be certain. Meduck and Cistoo making love would ruin all my plans.

Letodah was the only person in the tribe who could trump what the chief had to say. After all, had he not seen it in the tobacco he had tossed into the fire? The leaves crackled and flamed up magnificently when he asked the spirits if Cistoo would be the best choice as his apprentice. *Have not both my power animal and Upper World guide also confirmed it?*

He informed both the peace chief and the war chief that this was Cistoo's destiny. "The spirits have commanded me to make this shocking choice!"

The chiefs' jaws dropped. "But is this not the same girl who caused her own mother's illness and death? How could she be a good choice for shaman?"

Letodah predicted disaster visiting the tribe if the chiefs ignored his strong urgings. "There will be a great earthquake, sucking us all into the ground, if this order is disobeyed. I don't understand it either, making a young girl the next shaman for the tribe, especially this girl. But the spirits have wisdom we don't have ourselves. We are setting ourselves up for destruction if we ignore them."

The couple awaited Letodah's arrival on the morning of their wedding. They stood in the center of the village, surrounded by family and tribe. A large blanket held deer meat, apples, maize, and squirrel. There would be a feast and celebration after the official pronouncement. Cistoo wore a buckskin dress. Meduck wore black pants bought at the trading post, a white shirt, and a red sash around his head and waist.

Minutes before the ceremony, Cistoo whispered in Meduck's ear, "You are a very pretty bride."

Meduck giggled. "I agree." Bashful, he held his hand over his mouth.

Letodah walked out into the ring of people and stood in front of Meduck and Cistoo. To all present, it appeared that he was about to begin the official marriage ritual. Instead, his words shocked and disheartened both families: "There will be no marriage today or ever between these two."

The crowd turned to each other in disbelief. Had their shaman seen a bad sign that would prevent this union?

"In the days ahead, I will explain my decision, but as for now, I must tell you that it is not the will of the Great Spirit for this wedding to take place. An earthquake would swallow us up and destroy our village if we were to proceed. The chiefs have agreed with me and given their permission to stop this ceremony. Go back to your daily work. No marriage will take place today."

The families of the couple were sad, and their sadness exceeded the happiness they had felt about the wedding. But wanting to avoid disaster, they did as they were told.

Privately, Meduck shared with Cistoo, "I feel like a burden has been lifted from me. I don't have to live a double life now, pretending to be a hunter and a warrior. It's a relief."

The aunties and Meduck's parents, brothers, and sisters returned to their huts. The braves returned to their arrow making and games. Melauki walked alongside them. He always looked forward to weddings. The food was good, and he liked dancing. This time, though, he was beset by another feeling that surprised him. A gladness had settled on his heart, which he quickly dismissed as he returned to his ordinary duties.

Cistoo solemnly accompanied Letodah, but her heart danced, happily. Her fake marriage had been called off.

As soon as Letodah was alone with Cistoo, he told her the real reason he had stopped the ceremony. "You have a higher calling beyond the hunters and the warriors. You will be my apprentice. When I pass on to the Galun Lati, you will take over as the tribe's shaman."

Cistoo was so surprised, she gasped for breath. "Will you teach me everything you know?"

Letodah nodded. "Yes."

"I am honored above all the boys of the tribe to be chosen. Everyone has to respect me now."

Letodah told Cistoo what being a shaman would entail. "Being a shaman is not easy. It is a lonely job, especially when you don't have the whole tribe behind you. It means being set apart from the rest of the village. A shaman can never marry or lie down with a partner. A medicine man cannot have friends. He must be set apart from and above others. The shaman must be different because the tribe needs him to be. Tribe's people must believe that no ordinary person could bring the magic into their lives that the shaman brings. The shaman is unlike ordinary humans; he lives a special life. I am asking you if you are sure that you want to commit yourself to that life."

"Yes, I do, but didn't the Great Spirit choose me for this job?" she asked, puzzled.

"Yes, but you do have to cooperate."

"I am sure. I never imagined such a role for myself. I can think of nothing better. I am committed."

Cistoo was a shrewd girl. Instantly, she thought, *I will have the most power next to the chiefs and sometimes even more power than they will. When I replace Letodah, the chiefs will come to me for counsel.*

Cistoo had wondered what it would be like to be shaman. She had not dared to speak those words out loud, as that would have amounted to heresy. Braves were the ones who decided for themselves if they wanted to become medicine men. But she could not have decided this path for herself. The shamanic way had never been an option for a girl.

But when Letodah had been watching her, she had been watching him as well. She was fascinated by everything he did and keenly recalled every detail of every ceremony she had watched him perform. She had dared not share her desire to perform them with anyone. To share this desire would be a betrayal of her womanhood that no one in the tribe could abide.

Yet it had happened. *I can't believe this is happening to me. I never dared to think that anything so wonderful could come to pass.*

She hoped her father would finally hold her in high regard. *How can he turn away from me now? What parent wouldn't be proud of a child chosen for such a high honor? And a girl child at that! It has never happened before, ever.*

Cistoo flushed with warm anticipation every time she thought of it. She tripled her resolve. "I will work harder than anyone has worked before. When will you tell the rest of the tribe?" She hoped it would be soon.

"In a few days after they have had a chance to absorb the news about the marriage. This will be hard for them to accept. I must choose the right words."

The admiration she had felt for Letodah immediately transformed into a deep, abiding love. "You have saved me from keeping up a fake marriage to Meduck. I like Meduck, but to be tied to him for life? Waiting on him in public?" The idea of it made her shudder. "I am the real warrior between the two of us, aren't I?"

Suddenly she saw that marrying Meduck would have been a lifelong insult ultimately eroding her soul. She saw that fact with a clarity that had previously escaped her.

Cistoo felt overcome with gratitude toward Letodah. "Now you have saved me three times."

"It is your destiny," he answered confidently. "You have the chance to show the tribe what you can do. Our people do not know it now, but very soon they will need all the skills you possess."

Letodah was eager to train Cistoo. *She must be prepared to take over when I reunite with the Great Spirit. I will devote every bit of my soul's strength to teach her. The tribe will doubt me if I fail to train her well. I could become a laughingstock.*

Yet I always thought I would choose a boy. For years when he had imagined taking on an apprentice, he had envisioned the bright young face of a male. But he had not wanted to admit it fully to himself.

A week later, Letodah made the announcement that Cistoo would be his new apprentice. "Cistoo has more talent and gifts for shamanic medicine than I have ever seen in any of the males."

The audience gasped and talked among themselves nervously. A visiting tribal neighbor, Euchella's now Choctaw brother, had watched both the game and the canceled wedding from a healthy distance. At this news, he ran many miles back through the forest. When he arrived back at his village, he went straight to his chief's hut. "My Cherokee shaman, Letodah, has lost his mind. He has convinced their chief to make Cistoo his apprentice."

The Choctaw chief immediately called a tribal meeting. "The situation is too dangerous. Women must not be shamans. The whites will run over us if we sink to such a low level." His message resounded with the council. Their response was swift. Cistoo must be killed.

"The sooner the better."

Chapter 4

The Education

*C*istoo had bright hopes for her future.

Together she and Letodah built her a round lodging with a conical, bundled-stick roof. The dwelling set close to his on the edge of the village. A hole in the center of the roof allowed the smoke to rise from the fire pit in the middle of her dwelling. Mud held the sticks and roof together, which kept the wind and elements out. A squirrel skin covered the only entrance.

Cistoo filled her small but functional home with talisman plants, hides to make her comfortable, and tools that were necessary for her craft. She lay down at night on a deerskin the aunties had given her. They had also purchased an additional blanket from the nearest trading post. At night, Cistoo covered herself with the well-worn blanket she used as a child.

On their first day of training, Letodah took Cistoo into the woods to teach her to identify plants and herbs that had curative powers.

Why do I have to start in such a little girl's way? she wondered. She would have preferred learning one of the rituals she had seen Letodah perform, preferably involving fire and frenzied dancing. "I am used to being active like a hunter," she said. "Can we start by learning something less ... boring?"

"A plant saved your life, did it not? Now you do not want to learn about plants? Such ingratitude." The look in Letodah's eyes convinced Cistoo of her wrongheadedness. "Now you are being given the honor of learning how to save someone else," Letodah said sternly. Cistoo knew he was right.

The first plant Letodah showed her was one he employed often. Only specific parts of each plant were used. "Sometimes I use the bark; sometimes the bud is the potent part. At other times, I collect the roots or twigs. Healing through medicine plants is complicated."

Many of the plants could be identified initially by their smells. Some smelled bitter; others smelled sweet. Some even smelled like dirt.

"Be careful to leave the roots of the plant growing where you found them. You want the plant to be useful to you in the future when another person falls ill. That is how we keep a steady supply of medicine." Letodah cautioned her.

Letodah carried several tools with him: a sharp knife and a blade fashioned to a sturdy piece of wood for digging. "You will need to wash all your materials thoroughly in the stream after each use. You do not want the juices of several plants to mix together on your tools. The tool could be poisoned with different medicines coming together. That could cause the medicine to lose its power—or worse, make a person sick or dead."

"The plants themselves must be cleaned and dried after collecting them. Remove dirt particles and unwanted plant parts, or rocks sticking to the roots. If time will pass before you use the plant, dry it quickly with smoke. This will preserve its healing properties."

Of all the plants Letodah showed her that first day in the field, Cistoo's favorite smelled like peppermint. "This plant helps bellyaches," Letodah said. "It also helps people who can't eat. I use it too, when food backs up into a sick Indian's mouth, and he throws up the mess onto the ground."

The plants that Letodah showed Cistoo had a variety of uses. Many helped with burns from the sun or from fire. Others helped with insect bites, wounds, and poison ivy. "I will like helping people get well," she said. This knowledge touched a side of her that following her aunties' way had not. Neither had the way of the warrior brought her the calmness now settling within her.

Letodah told Cistoo that one of her aunties had a big pain in her head. "She called for me, but this is a chance for you to use your new knowledge."

Cistoo went to her auntie's hut, bearing the treasure of the new medicine.

"Cistoo, I am glad you are here, but I was expecting Letodah. I have been so sick, girl, I can't get off my pallet. Your other aunties have been doing all of my work. You know I don't like that."

"Don't worry, auntie. Letodah has sent me. He told me what you need."

Cistoo used the herb feverfew to cure her auntie. Within hours, she was able to get up and return to her duties.

The feverfew had a side effect as well. "You know, Cistoo, the medicine you gave me has helped to fix the aches in my hips."

"That benefit will only last a little while, auntie, but I'm glad it is helping for now."

"You are learning so much and so fast." Cistoo's auntie hugged her and gave her a big smile.

Young hunters soon enlisted Letodah to help them find fresh game. They had left camp four times in recent weeks and returned with nothing to show for their efforts. It was as if the animals had a secret pact to hide from all humans. Locating rabbit, deer, and squirrel, normally plentiful in the area, had become impossible. The prior winter had been especially harsh. Letodah guessed that many animals had perished from the extreme cold.

Even when game was spotted, the boys' aims had been poor. Plenty of arrows were shot; none of them struck home. With no new game killed for the tribe, resources in the village were low. Cistoo woke up early for the hunt. She could not believe her good fortune. She had a chance to prove to everyone that she was worthy. "We will bring back so much meat, they won't be able to eat it all, Father." *Letodah likes it when I call him Father,* she thought.

"We will try ... Daughter. We will try," he said gently.

Before leading the hunt, Letodah performed a tobacco ceremony to reveal where plentiful hunting could be found. Letodah threw leaves into a small fire, using the occasion to instruct his new apprentice in the art of reading smoke. Then he threw small amounts of tobacco into the fire three times. "The forecast is east. That is the direction where the game will be most plentiful."

With fascination, Cistoo watched the reading of tobacco flames.

Letodah elaborated. "This is one skill where you will find it helpful to be a female. Females naturally pay more attention to what their inner feeling is telling them. This inner feeling is called instinct. All animals have it, but it is still a mystery to the medicine men of bygone days. Men need much more training to learn to follow their instinct."

Letodah speculated further. "Instinct may be the reason the shamans did not allow women to be apprentices in the past. They could see that instinct was a power that women use naturally. When a woman's instinct joins with the shaman's skill of tobacco-leaf reading, women gain great power. Women start out with a strong advantage over men. The men are afraid that if they shared their skill with women, the men will look weak next to them."

That explanation seemed reasonable to Cistoo. She had witnessed that her aunties knew things about other people and animals. Males were often baffled, asking them how they knew such secrets. The men themselves did not see the clues. They needed more information to make correct judgments.

Cistoo knew she had this instinct. The thought of it made her feel a cut above her band of brothers. She liked that feeling, which excited her. She had ridden and hunted with the braves before when they had allowed it. Now she was on superior ground. She found this fresh aspect of their relationship impossible to keep to herself.

As she and Letodah rode their horses over to gather up the other half-dozen hunters, she barked the first orders: "Letodah and I will lead you to game. You will follow. Do as we say, and your aim will be true. Don't count on yourselves. On this trip, you must count only on Father Letodah, and me."

The braves bristled at these instructions. "Who do you think you are, girl?"

Letodah commanded them, "On this hunt, I want you to follow my orders and Cistoo's orders. She is second in command."

The braves knew they had to obey even if they didn't like it. Hearing these words from this girl stung. They knew how fit she was to ride with them, but they all agreed that she didn't have to be so happy rubbing it in.

Melauki sought to soften the blow. "Well, we didn't have any luck hunting on our own. Might as well follow Cistoo. We couldn't do worse."

The hunters, Letodah, and Cistoo took the rations that the aunties had prepared for them and rode off toward the nearest mountain and forest. Cistoo thrilled at the notion that she would be the provider rather than the receiver of the provisions. *I will be the savior of the tribe, along with Letodah, of course.* She did not think to include the other hunters in her fantasy.

The band of hunters rode all day toward the east. Since they had no luck hunting in the areas close to the camp, Letodah's instinct advised him to travel further. He felt led to this conclusion by his keenly developed instinct.

When twilight fell, they set up camp next to an embankment and a small stream. They tied up their horses, ate the dried meat, and lay down to sleep.

Suddenly, in the middle of the night, a sharp, unrecognizable bird cry awoke Cistoo. *Maybe a crow or a buzzard,* she thought. Yet the sound had an eerie quality that told her it was neither. She sat up, cocking her ear in the bird's direction. Now that she was a shaman's apprentice, she paid more attention to each sight and sound in her life. She knew this sound could be pointing her in a particular direction, but she didn't know where. Letodah had schooled her well. *I must not use my mind to decide what the sign means. The sound itself will lead me.* She got up and followed the clear, loud cawing.

Cistoo wondered how the men managed to sleep through the sound. *Must be my stronger instinct that woke me up,* she thought. *Or maybe I'm paying attention and they are not.* Like any young apprentice, she was eager to follow all of Letodah's recent lessons.

She followed the cawing for a short distance before sensing that the sound was now beside her. Still, she could not see the bird. Then she looked up. In a tall chestnut tree, she spotted a big, black bird. It turned its head downward and stared directly at her.

The bird communicated with her alone, speaking straight into her mind, though she could hear no words. "Follow me," it said.

The bird swooped down from the branch and flew ahead of her. *How will I keep up with it?* she worried.

Luckily, the full moon guided her. She could easily see the bird's path on the clear night. She saw it land on a small mountain outcrop maybe two miles away. She followed. Without questioning the wisdom of leaving the camp in the dead of night, she set out after the bird. No one else knew where she was going. No one else knew that she had even left. She simply trusted that this was the action she was to take.

She arrived at the scene where the crow-like animal landed. She saw it perch on a newly slaughtered deer. *I wonder how this deer was killed. There are no other hunters in the region.*

What do I do now? she asked herself. But the answer did not come. The bird offered no further instruction. Instead, sitting squarely on the deer carcass, it began to eat. It ate for a long time. After a while, the bird's black twin cawed and touched down on the fresh meat to feast as well.

Cistoo's instinct eluded her. The bird was too busy feeding to advise her. Since the moon had drifted behind clouds, she could not safely attempt to return to the camp. After the hard day's ride and this long walk in the middle of the night, she lay down exhausted. She gathered leaves around her for warmth. The autumn air provided a slight chill, but the winter cold had yet to settle in.

When the braves awoke the next morning, they followed their usual morning routine. They did not immediately notice that Cistoo was missing. They walked down to the small stream in the early morning and washed their faces and bodies. Letodah was the first to notice that his young apprentice no longer lay sleeping on her blanket. *Probably went to the stream to wash up with the others,* he thought.

But when Letodah went to the water and asked the young hunters, no one had seen her.

I hope she has avoided the beginner's mistake of believing that she knows more than she knows. Letodah quickly scanned the area around the camp while asking the braves to do the same. As soon as they were sure that she was nowhere in sight, Letodah knew they must search for her.

Looking at the space around her blanket, the men decided to follow the loose tracks she had left. "Why in the name of our ancestors would she leave like that? She doesn't know what she is doing. She has never been on a large hunt before." Perhaps part of the answer lay in the fact that she was a tenderfoot.

She didn't remember the number-one rule: stick together, no matter what.

"At least there are no animal tracks around her blanket." Letodah found slight reassurance in that fact. Visible animal tracks could mean that a mountain lion had dragged her off.

They ate their dried meat as they rode.

"Stupid girl." Melauki hissed under his breath.

"Watch your tongue!" Letodah snapped. He had sharp hearing. "She is one of your leaders."

Two hours later, the braves found Cistoo. She lay sleeping next to a small cliff cave under a shady tree. The sun had yet to waken her.

"Why did you run off on us?" Letodah demanded.

Cistoo rubbed her eyes and blurted out the night's adventures. She talked quickly in order to get the entire story out before Letodah chastised her further. "The bird sound—I don't know why the rest of you couldn't hear it, but I knew it was a sign. I knew I had to go after it."

"Where is this bird now?" Letodah was both amused and frustrated as well as touched with a hint of pride. *She is taking my lesson in instinct very seriously.*

Everyone looked around. No bird was within view, only the empty carcass of the deer. The two birds had made swift work, devouring half of the animal during the night.

The braves laughed, covering their mouths to avoid Letodah's criticism.

Then they heard a fresh noise—a deep, penetrating growl. With little time to react, they turned. A huge grizzly raced toward Melauki, grabbed him by the neck, and slammed him hard to the ground.

Shouting frantically at the bear, the braves threw stones and snatched up any available branch to try to save their brother. But it was Letodah's true aim, shooting a single arrow straight through the bear's head, that felled him.

Melauki lay seriously mauled. Deeply pitted claw prints ran down his back. Blood poured from his injuries. Cistoo knew they must get him back to camp fast so he could be treated. Letodah staunched the cuts with a fire stick to stop the bleeding. He assigned three men and Cistoo the job of taking Melauki back to the village. The men made a sleigh by lashing branches together in order to pull their brother back to his lodging.

"But I want to stay with you, Father," Cistoo pleaded. "I want to bring the bear back to camp, so we can show the tribe our successful hunt."

Letodah turned on her. She had never seen him so angry. "Because of your beginner's mistake, Melauki will probably die. Don't you see that? Go. Be where you belong. Be with the man you have led to this bear."

Letodah stayed with the three boys as they fashioned a sleigh on which to drag the huge bear. While the bear would feed the whole tribe for about a month, Letodah doubted that Cistoo's instinct had ruled her actions. She could have died herself. In fact, she should have died herself.

Why was it, he wondered, *that the bear had not come out in the night and dragged her to his cave. Why hadn't the bear come out and eaten the deer?* That aspect of the hunt would make this day something of a miracle—but only if Melauki survived.

Letodah believed that a shaman must follow the signs that the Great Spirit set out to guide him. *Only then,* he thought, *can a shaman come to the place where he is supposed to be. The way to the end point is fraught with danger and hardship. Maybe Cistoo was going a little on instinct and a little on shamanic knowing.* But he was too angry with her to admit to even a speck of truth in that idea.

Along with that thought, Letodah saw a glimmer of something else. For the first time with Cistoo, he was beginning to feel what he had to describe as love. *I hope those soft feelings don't mess with my powers. Damn, emotions will just get in my way. What have I done to myself?*

Cistoo and the braves dragged Melauki and the bear carcass back to the village on separate sleighs. When the band returned, the children snarled with delight as they danced around the grizzly. Their delight changed immediately into wails of fear over Melauki's grave condition. At once, the aunties made a clean bed for him next to the fire in the largest hut. He had been delirious and feverish during the trip. The brothers had given him water and kept his wounds clean. But his injuries were deep; the outcome of his treatment was far from certain.

The hunters worried for their brother, but they stayed strong. They knew that each hunt involved danger. Melauki's destiny had brought him face-to-face with the grizzly. This was a fact. They didn't blame Cistoo. Instead, they felt a gnawing awareness that she had led them to this bear. The bear meat would feed the tribe and prevent them from having to move from the camp—at least for a little while longer.

What actually happened passed everyone's expectations. This particular hunt seemed to break the bad spell hanging over the village. In the few weeks after the bear attack, they slaughtered enough deer, squirrel, and wild turkeys to feed the village for the entire winter. The tribe could stay put during the cruel season.

Melauki survived, but his recuperation was going to take months. With the medicine man's antibiotic plants and the aunties' loving care, slowly he began to heal. Even so, he had many scars from the bear's sharp claws. He liked the scars though—especially the jagged one across his right cheek. His back was covered with deep, crisscrossed grooves. He wore these marks as badges of honor that displayed his victory over death.

Cistoo did not want to visit him. She still stung from the painful words Letodah had spoken to her on the day of the bear attack. Yet she needed to talk with the man whose death she almost caused.

How could I have only been thinking of myself? She blushed inwardly with shame thinking that her first thought had been of being a hero. She did not know if she would recover from that shame.

Two weeks after the hunt, she walked to the hut where Melauki lay, to beg for his forgiveness. Timidly, Cistoo approached him. He was still too weak to get up and move around; but he could carry on a conversation, if it didn't last too long. Talking wore him out.

"I am sorry you got hurt so bad by that bear."

"Me too. But I like the scars. The next bear I meet will be scared of me."

Cistoo laughed. "So are we still friends?"

"We were never friends, Cistoo. But if you want to know if I hold it against you, no, I don't hold it against you."

"Thank you."

"But you have more to worry about than what I think of you."

"What do you mean?"

"Even lying here I have heard the news that a lot of Indians are angry about Letodah making you shaman."

Cistoo shrugged. "That's too bad." She paused. "But I don't care. Most people in the tribe have shunned me my whole life. Why should I care what they think? The chief agreed to it. The Great Spirit would bring an earthquake on our village if Letodah didn't choose me. They have no choice."

"You are such a baby. You should know by now that nothing is easy. Half the tribe is trying to figure out what to do about you."

"That means half the tribe is for me. They must see my skills."

"You are so stupid sometimes. Our tribe is breaking apart because of you. I don't think you're safe."

"Why would someone want to hurt me?"

"How can you act surprised? Your cousins almost killed you."

"Do you think I deserve to be shaman?"

"I think that is for the Great Spirit to decide. He talks to Letodah more than he talks to me."

"Letodah has said nothing about this to me."

"Go talk to him. I want to sleep now."

"I'll go talk to him"

"Go now. You have to deal with this before something bad happens to you. You should think about it. Maybe you are bad luck."

"I am a shaman. A shaman in training, but still a shaman. No matter what some people say."

Cistoo walked the short distance back to her hut. Letodah sat inside waiting for her.

"Tell me what we are going to do, Father? Melauki has said we are about to have an uprising in our tribe."

"We are meeting together tonight in the deciding circle. Indians from both sides will gather. The tribe will probably split."

"Over me?"

"Yes."

"Are you sorry you chose me?" Cistoo felt genuine fear. She did not want to lose Letodah's support. Most of all she did not want to lose her new role.

"I will be honest. I have had moments of doubt, especially when you led us to that bear. But, no, I am sure that I have chosen wisely. I want to do what the Great Spirit wants."

They talked about what they would say at the meeting. Letodah would do the talking. Cistoo would stay silent. He instructed her not to defend herself.

In Cistoo's village, both the peace chief and the war chief met to discuss her fate. Thirty council members gathered around a large fire. About an equal number represented each side of the debate. They passed the pipe to signal this was to be a peaceful talk. The chiefs decided that the Indians who opposed Cistoo should speak first.

The war chief began. "We know Letodah has powerful medicine. But maybe he misinterpreted the message he received about making Cistoo shaman. Look at the facts. Her mother caught her sickness and died. Her father believes she carries a curse. Her own relatives tried to kill her. And now, on her first hunt as an apprentice, one of our best braves is almost killed by a bear. Cistoo led the hunters to the bear. Why do we think she should be shaman? Everything that has happened in her life shows what bad luck she is."

Another brave spoke up. He had played in the games with Cistoo and gone on the hunt as well. "She is a strange girl. She can barely do what a woman is made to do, but she wants to have power to guide our tribe. She is more boy than girl. That worries me."

The representative from the women took a turn. "Look at what is happening to our tribe already over her. We lost nine tribe members when Euchella's relatives left on account of her. Now we are thinking of dividing again and reducing our strength to smaller numbers. Nothing that she has touched so far has helped anyone."

Letodah asked for and received permission to speak. "There are things you do not know about this girl. I have been watching her for years. It was her mother's choice to take on the worst of the illness and die instead of losing her daughter. I was there. Her mother's spirit spoke to me. Euchella shunned his daughter because he was crazy with grief. His relatives left because they tried to kill her."

"You are making excuses!" The war chief was adamant.

"I am speaking facts. Cistoo can run faster, shoot straighter, and ride harder than any brave in the tribe. She has great instinct. Leading us to the bear only seems bad at first. When you look at it more deeply, the truth is our food supply has improved. Has not the spell been broken on our poor hunting season?"

"Melauki might have an opinion on this!"

The crowd turned to hear the voice speaking from behind the gathering. The women caring for Melauki had dragged him on a blanket out to the gathering.

"Melauki thinks that Cistoo should be shaman," he said. "I do not want to say this in front of everyone, but she is better at everything than I am. And I am truly excellent. Letodah speaks for the Great Spirit. If we do not listen to him, we dishonor our God and put ourselves in great danger."

"How do we know this is not your sickness speaking?" the war chief asked.

"Because I make the best sense of anyone here."

The war chief started to rise from this insult when the white trader, Tom Jessup, ran into their midst led by one of their Indian guards. Jessup had made regular trips to the tribe to trade food for pelts.

"You'd not want yer women and children to suffer the same fate as the ones in the village I jes' passed. Everythin' was burnt to ashes. Bodies layin' aroun' every which a-way. Whites takin' scalps like they was Injuns. It stunk so bad I threw up right there in the dirt. I heard that the only people they didn't kill were some sturdy lookin' women and children. I guess they're gonna pass 'em off for slaves." Jessup's hat and clothes were covered with filth and vines from running through the forest.

Hard to imagine dead bodies smelling worse than him. Cistoo thought as she worried. *What's going to happen to us?*

Cistoo was no longer the center of attention. The chiefs had to decide their course of action in response to this slaughter.

The year was 1810. Cistoo's tribe had had little involvement with the whites so far—either by trading or by fighting with them. Her tribe had chosen to remain separate. Up until that point, it had worked for them. Living in a mountain valley, they had a natural kind of isolation. Unlike other tribes, they were harder to get to, so they were harder to attack. Yet they all knew that the day would come when they might have to defend their land. That day had arrived.

The war chief offered an aggressive solution. "Why don't we gather our best warriors, hunt the whites down, and kill them?

We will surprise them by hitting first. We will strike fear in their hearts. They will retreat. They will not dare to occupy our lands, knowing how easily we can annihilate them."

A third of the men supported fighting. Others were not so quick to jump to this approach.

An elderly man spoke up. "Going to war is not practical or helpful over a long period of time. Indians have gotten used to trading with whites. White men have goods that Indians want: guns, horses, ammunition, blankets. And the more we learn, the more we discover what else might be useful to us. Maybe it would be wiser to trade with the whites than kill them. Maybe we should try a peace talk."

The war chief argued, "That attack on the village is not giving us any option to trade with the whites. This is about more than trading with the whites. We are giving up the way we have lived for centuries. We have lived well, with joy, on our land without the whites. We have counted only on ourselves to survive. If we depend on the invaders to give us what we need to live, we will lose who we are. We will not be Indians anymore. We will be white men with white men's spirits. The Cherokee would look the same on the outside, but inside we would be changed for good."

Melauki agreed with the war chief, while others thought that he was going way over the edge in his argument.

Others said they wanted to make their lives easier.

Meduck said, "We have lived hard. Our lives are full of work. We have to work for everything. They have time to make what they call music. I heard it when I came near a white village. It is amazing. Hearing it made my body want to move. We have our drums and the birds' singing, but if you heard this music, you would want to dance."

Another Indian in the gathering could not conceive of this music. It made him angry to hear of it. "I have not heard music. But it sounds like something a lazy man would do with his time.

Why are you bringing this up now when we're trying to decide how to save our lives?"

The peace chief stood up and spoke for the first time. "We must have a plan that we all agree on. Our tribe counts on us to stay alive."

The men talked about different approaches that the Indians might take toward the rapidly approaching whites. Finally, the decision was made to leave the area.

The peace chief supported this opinion. "War is hard to back away from. Once war is begun, many winters could pass before trust between our people returns. Neither side gains when war is going on."

Letodah was consulted for the Great Spirit's guidance on how to approach the encroaching whites. He cast tobacco into the fire to determine what the strongest direction would be for the Indians to take. The reading suggested taking a peaceful approach.

"The leaves favor peace." *But what does that mean?* Letodah thought. *We can be peaceful by staying or by leaving.*

"Voting for peace plays into the hands of the whites. It flies in the face of reality," Cistoo blurted out. "Treaties haven't worked before, and the whites are attacking us again."

Cistoo knew that she was not supposed to speak, but she could not hold back her opinion. When she saw Letodah glaring at her, she shut up immediately.

He said, "I know a way we can deal with the white invaders and decide about Cistoo as my apprentice at the same time. If we are going to split apart anyway, why not split now? Half of us who believe in Cistoo can go together. The other half can go its own way."

"But, Letodah, we are already a small tribe. Won't that make us easy targets if the whites catch up with us?"

"Not if we have a plan."

Cistoo could barely tolerate what she was hearing. Her intuition told her that the white men moving toward their territory forced the Cherokee to fight. But she must go along with her chief and her shaman.

Under her breath, she gave her real opinion. "It is disastrous for our people to seek peace."

Chapter 5

Retreat

As Jessup had described it, whites had taken up the Indian practice of scalping their victims. "Them whites wanna keep a count a how many Injuns they kilt."

After Jessup, runners from other tribes and white traders fluent in Cherokee passed through Cistoo's village. They too brought with them ghastly stories of whole villages massacred by the whites.

Indians and whites had different philosophies of battle. While the Indian tribes often attacked one another, attacks were brief. The idea was to maintain balance. If one or more of their tribesmen were killed by a neighboring tribe, then the assaulted tribe had the right to counterattack the offending tribe and kill the same number of tribesmen. In that way the "score" was kept even, or balanced.

The white men, however, were interested in destroying their enemies. Their philosophy was to leave little or nothing behind on which the survivor could build. Burn tents and clothes, steal horses, guns, and utensils, rape and kill women and children or sell them into slavery.

The chiefs, Letodah, and the rest of the tribal council decided on a plan.

The peace chief informed the whole tribe. "Indians have been on this land for hundreds of years, but survival now means leaving the village behind us. This land has given us much. But we must take our women and children to safety. Our tribe will leave in two groups. But later we will split, about half going with Letodah, Cistoo, and the peace chief and the other half going with the war chief. "

A group of seventy-three woman and children would leave first.

"Cistoo, you will leave with the women and children in canoes," Letodah said. "Three men will travel with you. I will stay behind to lead the second group. The chiefs will come on horseback with me on land beside the river. The men will protect the women and children going before them."

"I don't want to go without you," she said.

"It is necessary. If attackers follow us, the men will be there to defend you. We will start several days behind you."

"I will do as you say, Father," Cistoo agreed reluctantly. "I will ask the Great Spirit to protect us."

"I also want to follow you so that Euchella can come with us. I know when he is around it is easy for you to doubt yourself. For this journey, you will need to believe in yourself as a true leader, because you are."

Letodah continued. "The men with you will choose the spot where you are to set up camp. There is land in both Tennessee and Arkansas where we can be safe, at least for a time. By water it will take about five weeks to make the trip."

Cistoo told her group to gather as many rations as they could carry in the canoes. "We will feed ourselves with what we bring. And we will add to it by fishing, hunting, and berry picking along the way."

The children were running around, acting more wild than usual. Uprooted from the only home they had known since birth, they had little understanding of what was happening. Cistoo had offered comfort to the children by telling them the Nunnehi would also be watching out for them.

A small girl asked, "What do the Nunnehi look like?"

"Well ..." Cistoo squatted to make herself the same height as the child. "What the Nunnehi look like depends on whether they are a boy or a girl. They are all small, no more than four to eight hands high. The men all have long, gray beards down to their toes. They like to wear colorful hats. The men's voices sound like thunder.

"The women are more delicate, very pretty, like you. When they speak, their words remind you of a gentle waterfall. The women, though, can be dangerous. If you are a boy, I tell you never to fall in love with a strange girl you meet in the forest. If a boy kisses a Nunnehi, he falls under her spell forever. His free spirit is lost for good.

"Even when the Nunnehi help us find our way, you should be careful getting near one. They are tricky. You need to fear them. Always show them great respect, and feed them whatever you have. They like being fed. They have big appetites and are always hungry. There is never a time when a Nunnehi has had enough to eat.

"You are still a child and may yet see one."

The little girl took all of the information in soberly, saying, "I hope I don't have to wait long to see one." Clearly, what Cistoo had said about the *Yvnwi Tsunsdi* had not scared this child even a little bit.

Cistoo smiled. The girl reminded her of herself. Another reminder to be a great shaman—she would serve as a model for all the females to come.

Talking to the little girl took Cistoo back to when she and her mother had talked when she was a little girl. She went to visit her mother's grave. For all she knew, this would be her last visit to the site for a very long time. She did not know if she would ever return.

"Oh, Mother, I am leaving you. It makes me so sad. You see everything from the Galun Lati. You know we are in danger. We must go. There will be no one here to guard your grave. But I will pray for your protection with the Great Spirit. I pray that someday I can return to keep this holy ground safe. Please bless us, Mother. You will come with me in spirit to keep me company. I do not want you to be lonesome."

A few of the braves objected to the decision to move, but the war chief was adamant. "To stay on the property and defend it against attackers is too risky. It is true that the terrain makes it harder for attackers to make a surprise attack. But once they have reached us, we would be outnumbered. We would be unable to shield ourselves. We would be wiped out."

The first group to leave included forty-seven women, twenty-three children, and three braves in five longboat canoes. Extra canoes had been built in preparation for the departure. The canoes were kept in good repair, ready to board on short notice.

Every able woman and child served as rowers. Many were trained after they got into the boat. "Tilt the oar as you put it into the water. You want to row together. You want to avoid splashing and short little strokes." It took a while, but by midday, the rowers were in sync.

They rowed all day down the river. At sunset, they rowed to the banks and turned over their canoes. To avoid lighting the way to their position, they cooked very little by fire. The group departed in mid autumn, so the night chill in the air felt mild. The leaves had recently turned red, orange, and yellow. Women and children huddled together to sleep under blankets and leaves.

Adults took turns at lookout. Even the females and older male children participated in the lookouts. They doubted that anyone would follow them yet. No one could know they had left. Maintaining a constant vigil would be a smart strategy.

"I will take the first lookout," Cistoo said, for she took her leadership role seriously. Assuming the first watch reassured her sense that the camp was secure for the night.

The next day, rain on the river brought a torrential downpour. Using clay bowls, boys and girls were initially able to bail the water out of the canoe as fast as it poured in. Soon, though, the rain fell so hard the canoes began to fill up. Cistoo called out, "Row to the banks. Row to the banks as fast as you can."

The crew followed her order, rowing quickly to the riverbank. They emptied the water and sat with the canoes over their heads until the deluge slowed down. When the sun emerged from behind the clouds, their clothes dried quickly as they continued to row.

Cistoo knew to expect rushing rapids on the third or fourth day of the journey. The rough waters would be the toughest leg of the journey. The canoes would pass through an extended flow of them.

Cistoo instructed her rowers before reaching the rock-laden rapids. "Turning quickly is the skill we will need with those waters. You must keep one oar still while paddling rapidly with the other. To turn you must go in different directions with the different paddles. Or you can keep one paddle still in the water while taking the other out."

The crews practiced these techniques many times before reaching the rapids. It still required them to gather all their strength to navigate successfully around the rocks.

Cistoo yelled out the commands when she first spotted the rapids at a distance. "Move the canoe holding the supplies to the middle of the pack. These boats hold most of the jerky and other foods. Put the other canoes around it so it's less likely to hit the rocks."

The supply boat moved into the middle of the pack, but it still slammed into a jagged rock, ripping a hole in the bow. The rowers of the canoe traveling alongside the supply boat grasped the damaged front bow until they could safely guide it to shore. This was the closest that the canoe had come to being lost. Losing those supplies would have severely curtailed their journey. They would have had to settle sooner than they had anticipated. If they'd had to stop, they would not have distanced themselves enough from the advancing colonists.

The travelers spoke little, only when they had to convey some practical information to one another, such as "Tear me a piece of jerky or be quiet. We don't want to call attention to ourselves." The children knew to stay quiet, but they got into arguments.

It was hard for them to be confined to the canoes for hours every day. "Can't we stop for a little while and run around in that field?" Of course, the parents had to say no. They couldn't take the chance of stopping, even for a short while.

When the days were sunny and warm, the slow glide down the river felt serene and easy. Sometimes the children fell asleep. Cistoo felt calm too, on those days. She felt the burden of leadership lighten on mornings that were placid and mild. She noticed that the reverse was true. If she doubted herself, if she felt unwell, if she felt frustrated, her inner discombobulation matched her surroundings. No matter how sunny the day, she would complain about it.

She marveled at this insight, thinking, *I wonder which has the greater sway over me, my surroundings or my mood.* She concluded that she must exert as much control over her inner feelings as possible. *I have a big responsibility. I must stay steady and focused. Many people depend on me to keep them alive.* Rain or sun, warm or cold, no matter which, eventually an attack would come. She needed to be prepared.

Yet she was happy to lead. She felt born to it. *I like making important decisions. I like people looking up to me.* Even as a child, she had experienced a peculiar inner strength that almost no other human could shake. Her father was the sole person who could make her wonder if she deserved this role.

Cistoo's company had been traveling for several weeks. Following their usual routine, they set up camp in a wooded, concealed area. It was early evening, about an hour before sunset. Every tribe's person, male and female, had learned how to read the signs in the sky—the shifts in lighting, the smells in the air, the positions of the sun—in order to determine the time of day. They also knew about the shorter times of daylight in the fall and winter months.

Cistoo offered teachings to the children at night before sleeping. "The Great Spirit designed the seasons in order to allow the crops more time to grow, more sun time during planting season. In the cold time, some animals go into hiding and sleep. They eat all spring and summer to fatten themselves up for long periods of rest. They don't need to eat when they are resting."

After many hours of rowing during the day, the people were ready to have a quick, light meal before going directly to sleep. As was her custom, Cistoo took first duty for a few hours until the moon assumed its highest position in the sky. Then one of the men would take over her shift. Her shift was nearly over when she heard a twig snap in the woods to the southeast of the camp. She had experience with night sounds and the sounds of animals scurrying through the forest. She could tell the difference between an animal breaking a stick and a human foot stepping on one. *This is surely the sound of a human foot,* she thought.

Quickly she woke up the next person on watch. "Tell the others we may need to leave in a hurry. Tell them to stay completely still and quiet."

Tomahawk in her fist, she stood ready for hand-to-hand combat. Barely inside a dense thicket, she heard another twig snap, followed within seconds by the sound of yet another snap.

This human being must want to be heard, or else he's too stupid to avoid it. No Cherokee would make so much noise—especially not over and over. Then it dawned on her. *Maybe this Cherokee is cracking the twigs on purpose.*

As soon as the thought entered her mind, a male figure stepped out from behind the shadowy trees. His features were hard to make out in the darkness.

"I'm standing so close to you, Ulvnotisgi Ageyutsa, you crazy girl. You are lucky I am not a bear." Instantly, Cistoo recognized Melauki's voice.

Cistoo covered her mouth with her hand, stifling a laugh. "What are you doing here, Melauki? You are supposed to be days behind us with Letodah's group."

"First tell me, did I not scare you, at least a little?"

"Don't be stupid," Cistoo countered. "You are lucky you don't have this tomahawk buried in your head." She would admit no fear.

Melauki continued. "Letodah sent me ahead to give you a message. Your company should not stay in Tennessee. Arkansas is much friendlier to the Cherokee. The great white soldier Jackson used the Cherokee for his war with the French. Then he threw them away. He showed no respect. Now he encourages the citizens of Tennessee to reject our people. Letodah and the chiefs have decided that our best destination is Arkansas."

"Are you here to help us with the new direction?" Cistoo believed she could find her way to Arkansas without him.

"I've been walking all day and night for several moons to catch up with you. I need sleep now. I am still not quite as strong as I used to be. When we wake up in the morning, we will decide on the next leg of our journey."

Cistoo led Melauki quietly to the edge of the campsite and gave him blankets. She signaled with the safe whistle that all was well.

"It was only Melauki." She said to the watchperson who had taken over her shift. Then she lay down to sleep, excited about the prospect of heading directly for Arkansas.

Her mind raced. *We'll be on the river longer now, at least another three weeks.* She was surprised that only a few difficulties had arisen. *Some bad weather, a few easy-to-remedy cuts and bruises, and several mild illnesses—but I don't know what we'll find in Arkansas.*

Arkansas territory seemed to be fairly peaceful. She knew that Arkansas was not in imminent danger of attacks from white colonists. Significant numbers of white colonists had not yet pushed that far west to shove Indians out of their own territory. In this situation, the Cherokee would be entering territory largely populated by other tribes. Some of the stories she had heard made her worry.

We must find a way to occupy this land together peacefully. Even though we have used such methods in the past, I don't want our tribe to push our Indian brothers and sisters out of their space. We want to come in peace and live in peace for the rest of our lives.

They wanted peace for the children and for generations to come. Otherwise, they would have stayed at home and fought. They would have not attempted to improve their lives by leaving their longtime home in Western North Carolina.

The women and children with Cistoo's group arose at first light. This day they were in for a treat. A few of the older boys had caught some fish from the nearby river to cook for breakfast. They made a fire pit with very hot wood embers that would emit little smoke, and it was mostly covered by the morning's food. Cooking the fish quickly rendered it crispy on the outside—a favorite, particularly among the children.

The musky fish smell floating in the air woke the children. The boys and girls danced around the fire in delight.

"I'm glad I found some way to please the children," Cistoo told Melauki. "This journey has been hard on them."

The next day Melauki gave Cistoo the rest of the message. "The long-term plan is to head for Arkansas. The current encampment you made will do until the rest of the company arrives with Letodah. There is room enough for all of us. We need to scout the immediate area to set up a larger camp for a few months."

This decision to bring a sudden halt to their journey perplexed Cistoo. "I would prefer to stay on the move, Melauki. It makes more sense to me. We would put more distance between us and the whites. Besides, I am used to being on the move. As long as we are on the move, I feel like we are making progress. Staying here feels like defeat."

"Don't worry, Cistoo. We are many, many days from our previous home. The whites will not realize that we are gone for quite a while. No one should come looking for us, because they have no reason to. All they are interested in is our land. They will have that. As soon as they have the land, any concern they had about us will disappear."

Melauki's explanation made sense. Yet the new plan handed a difficult reality to Cistoo. She had to wrestle with it alone. The vision that she had been following, with great focus and dedication, had changed. Now she must change both her plans and her direction.

I hear what Melauki is saying, and I will follow the chief's orders, but it still frustrates me. I've got to get my mind around this new plan. Not only that, but as a leader, I must pass the wisdom of taking this new direction on to our tribe. They were all committed to the earlier way.

Melauki, Cistoo, and one brave extended their scouting expedition up to ten miles on both sides of the river. They looked for a spot near the riverbank. Melauki said, "We do not want a traveler coming down the river to see our camp from the water. The tribe will build lookouts high up in the trees. Scouts sitting in them can spy an enemy when he is still far off."

Seven miles beyond the place where they had camped, Cistoo and Melauki discovered a good site on the river's east side that exhibited many needed features. It was close to the water but not visible from it; the river would be a source of drink, food, cleanliness, and transport. All benefited the village. This would be the first time their village sat by the water. Their previous camp had been a good meandering mile from the water through dense brush. While good for survival, it was not nearly as desirable and fortunate as this new site. The site they chose lay somewhere near the Tennessee/Arkansas border.

Letodah and his crew had run into big trouble on their journey to reach them. His group followed several days behind Cistoo's crew to ensure no one was following them. They were the protective shield in case the whites were to attack them. What actually happened, they had never anticipated.

Letodah's group contained mostly braves and a few women brought along to prepare the meals. In all, there were about eighty-seven Indians. The women were preparing a stew at twilight when six Indians ran hollering from the woods toward them. "Ya, ya, ya, ya, ya, ya, ya!" Their war cry took everyone off guard.

"You should have listened to us when you had the chance. There she is." The leader pointed to a young woman standing near the river. He ran over to her and firmly planted a hatchet in her neck. "No one else has to die. We have done what we came to do."

But Letodah's group would not let such a brazen attack go unanswered. One of their women had been murdered. They swarmed their attackers with knives and hatchets pulled, killing them all within minutes. A brave from Letodah's group also lay dead.

They dragged the bodies back into the woods. Letodah held up a torch over the faces of the dead. "I know who these people are. These are Euchella's brothers and cousins. They came to kill Cistoo."

Letodah and the second crew of tribespeople arrived in the temporary campsite a week after Melauki had shared his directive with Cistoo. Upon his arrival, the shaman saw that about half the new camp had been set up. The group, composed mostly of women and children, had done a good job of creating lean-tos. The company all were next to each other, covered by a common roof composed of sticks, mud, and leaves. Huddled together at night for warmth, they rid themselves of the need for a fire.

The season was slightly chilly after dark. If the tribe decided to stay longer than a month, however, they would have to build individual huts. Negotiating the winter while generating as little fire as possible would be a daunting task.

"Before we sleep, Cistoo, I must tell you what has happened," Letodah said. "Your father's brothers and cousins attacked our camp. Two of our people were killed—one brave and a young woman. The leader shouted out, 'There she is!' before killing her. It was one of Euchella's cousins. He must have thought she was you."

Cistoo gasped, horrified to hear about this young woman's death. She was only a little older than herself. "Why, Father? Why do they hunt me like this?" She was shocked by the lengths Euchella's relatives would take to get rid of her.

"They may have learned that I made you my apprentice. They would disapprove of any woman being a shaman. They hate you so much, they would never allow you to be a shaman."

"Do you think my father knew about these plans?"

"No, I don't think your father knew what he was starting when he told his relatives to shun you. Now he is too crazy from drunkenness to know anything or to do anything."

"Where is my father? I did not see him arrive with your group."

"He is back at the trading post, where he knows he can get his hands on firewater."

Letodah's response did not surprise her.

"What do we do now? Do you think more Indians will come after me?"

"I don't know. This fight is coming from Euchella's family. They are running out of people. They may think they succeeded in killing you. No one returned to carry the message, so I don't know if the ones who are left will have any reason to come after you. But we can't take that chance. We must get back on the river again tomorrow."

The tribe decided to split into two groups. The side supporting Cistoo as shaman would leave together. Those who opposed Cistoo's leadership would go their own way. This was the original plan, but they were being forced to execute it sooner than they had anticipated.

All the work the women and children had accomplished had to be torn down, leaving no trace that their tribe had ever been there. The groups would still travel by canoes, but they would part company in several days when the river divided in lower Tennessee.

Within a day, the bands were ready to set out again. It was especially hard on the children, who had enjoyed playing in the dead leaves on dry ground.

After Letodah had an opportunity to rest from his several-hundred-mile journey, he met with Cistoo. "How have you done with this latest test of your leadership?"

"It's been hard, but I was ready for it, thanks to your training—particularly the teaching you gave me about following the stars and the positions of the moon and sun."

"You have grown since we last spoke. When we arrive at our next stop, I will give you more knowledge. I must teach you fast. You will absorb all the teaching I can give you. As the situation is now, you will need it."

The groups rowed for several weeks and parted at the splitting of the river. Cistoo's group rowed another several weeks before deciding on a good place to stop. They were inside Arkansas.

For the time being, they set up camp at a spot that looked like a protected area. They were protected by dense tree cover, so they could not be seen from the river. They had yet to scout a more permanent area. Still, Letodah felt the next phase of Cistoo's training was very important. It must begin immediately.

She awoke before dawn, cleansed herself in the river, and met Letodah at a spot they had arranged the previous day. Melauki would handle any problems that might arise in the company. He would direct any other practical affairs that might come up.

Letodah's recent brush with death had added to his sense of urgency. "I want to train you as completely and quickly as I can"

Cistoo found the thought of living without Letodah sad, but eventually she would step fully into his moccasins. *I hope that day is very far away.* "I understand, Father. I know how important your teaching is. How will we start?"

"I will drum as you lie still. You will travel to the Underworld, where you will meet your power animal. The power animal is your guide in that world as well as in the Middle World where we live."

As Cistoo lay on the dry ground listening to the drumbeat, Letodah instructed her. "Lie still, close your eyes, and imagine a hole on the earth's surface. You will use it to tumble down to the Lower World. Once you arrive in the Lower World, explore the terrain for creatures who offer to be your guide."

Cistoo cleared her mind, focusing only on the steady beat of the drum. Within a few minutes, in her mind's eye, she saw a tree on the hillside with a large hole in the trunk. She could not tell if she was dreaming or if she actually saw the tree and the hole. She walked over to the hole and looked down. Leaning forward, her body tipped, and she found herself falling down the hole. She tumbled head over feet for what seemed like a long time before spilling out onto an altogether unfamiliar landscape.

She looked around in wonderment. The sky was a pale orange-red. Brown, purple, and gray mountains sat in the distance of the dry, rocky desert. No internal sense of direction guided her, so she walked straight ahead. She heard the beating of the drum; after a while, it synchronized itself with the beating of her heart. She sniffed the air, which held a fruity sweetness she identified as a smell akin to peaches.

In the distance, she saw movement, but she could not discern what was causing it. As she walked across the sand, she realized that she had a different sense of motion than usual. Her relationship to the mountains and terrain around her changed much faster than they would have in the Middle World. She was able to cover a far greater distance in a shorter time.

Her frame of reference changed rapidly in accord with each movement. First, the mountains were ahead of her. Then they were to her right. Then they sat to her left. It was confusing, but she was free from worry.

She looked at her hands. They looked the same as they always did to her, except that they looked dazzling and bright. They looked like her hands, but they also looked like the best hands, the ultimate hands. These were the hands that shaped and molded her life and the lives of everyone around her in one way or another.

Cistoo was distracted by a rush of wind past her on the right. The wind pushed her in the direction of a craggy cliff. She noticed a large bird's nest resting on it. She could see that there were eggs settled into the middle—five of them, five large eggs. She heard the babies cry out, "Wheet, wheet."

I wonder where the mother is. She should come back soon. Those eggs need sitting on.

The moment the thought appeared in her head, an eagle swooped down to spread her wings as she sat on her charges. Cistoo looked into the eyes of the mother eagle. Their minds melded. Instantly, Cistoo realized that she had found her power animal. This animal would guide her in her shamanic journey. She and the mother eagle stayed in place for what seemed like an eternity, fixed on each other's gaze.

The eagle is transferring her knowledge to me. Now I know what she knows. How else can you guide me, eagle?

Her power animal also possessed the intimate knowledge of who Cistoo was in her essence. Cistoo had the sense that she was being nurtured in a way that she remembered only when her mother had been alive. Her aunties had done their best, but try as they might, they could not duplicate the love of her mother, Nannuht.

For the first time since before her desperate illness, she felt an all-encompassing love; it was coming from the heart of the eagle mother. A wounded piece of her, which she had only partially recovered, emerged fully and was healed in that moment. Her power animal had begun to work its magic on her being.

Another emanation coming from her power guide gave the next direction Cistoo should take in the Underworld. The mother eagle instructed her so that she instantly knew when their gaze should break off: *Head next in the direction where my wing points.*

Cistoo followed the eagle's instruction until she came to the bottom of a hill. It was a low-lying spot where a red tent sat. The area looked breezy and comfortable. Under the tent sat a bed covered with woven blankets. Cistoo walked into the space. The strong energy of well-being pulled her into a healing vortex.

Mother Eagle communicated. *This is the place in your journeying where you should bring the gravely ill spirit bodies for healing.*

Thank you. Cistoo felt great gratitude to Mother Eagle. She needed this place. She could bring the sick there to receive the healing energy that they needed. She also knew that although everyone she brought here would be healed, some would live and some would die.

If it is the Great Spirit's will for a person to die, then the healing means accepting the approaching death. They will know that death is the beginning not the end. The dead will return to their original spirit selves in the Galvladi tsosv.

The time came to return to the tunnel that had brought her to the Underworld. The drumming grew louder as she approached the opening. She crawled inside and immediately began to tumble up toward the Middle World. In an instant she found herself lying on the ground, with Letodah still seated next to her, his eyes closed, drumming a steady beat.

She opened her eyes.

"Tell me about your journey." Letodah's drumbeats grew slower and slower, before slowing to a stop.

Cistoo spoke of the sights and sounds she had experienced to Letodah. She told him of her strong perception about the mother eagle. "I believe that the mother eagle is my power animal." Then she told him of the place of healing the mother eagle had led her to discover.

Letodah seemed pleased. He nodded reassuringly as she spoke.

They sat in silence for a time after her recounting before Letodah said, "A good first journey, Daughter. But you will know for certain that the mother eagle is your power animal only when you have that fact confirmed for you in this world."

"How will I know that, Father? I felt so sure that it must be so when I was in the Underworld."

"It may be so, or it may be leading you to your true power animal on this plane. You must stay alert for proof in your surroundings. Proof will come in the form of signs."

Vague advice, Cistoo thought. But she was used to it. *This is the shaman's way. I have to trust it.* She had grown to trust it more than she had in the beginning. At first, Letodah's lack of clarity had been foreign and unsatisfying to her.

"In a few days," Letodah added, "you will journey to the Upper World to find your guide in that realm. Between the Upper World and Lower World guides, you will be helped to bring balance to this middle plane where we exist."

Cistoo found that she needed a few days to absorb the intense experience she'd had in visiting the Underworld. During that time, although she had remained as alert as possible, she received no further confirmation of the mother eagle as her power animal.

On the third day after her trip to the Underworld, Letodah told her, "Now you must travel to the Upper World to find your guide there. This guide will be vital in your work. This guide will help you make smart plans."

Her first journey had proven to be extremely satisfying, so Cistoo looked forward with great excitement to visiting the Upper World. Letodah chanted and drummed, with Cistoo lying quietly on the earth. Several hours passed before he began to instruct her on the path to the Upper World. "You need to attract more calmness to yourself before traveling. If you are not calm, you will be in danger of upsetting your spirit's balance. Too much excitement will slow this process and interfere with how you see the Upper World. Your mind could easily fool you and take you off on a bad detour."

Letodah waited until her body and mind were in a calm state before completing his explanation of how to journey to the Upper World. "For this journey, you will find a tool that you will use to rise to the Upper World. Make your choice with ease, naturally. Just look deep into your mind's eye, and the image will come to you."

Cistoo saw a ladder into the clouds that drew her like a magnet to climb it. She visualized herself walking over to the rungs and stepping up. She passed through clouds punctuated by blue skies before arriving at a landscape completely unfamiliar to her. *I don't know where I am. I have never seen a place like this. How will I know how to get around?*

Swirls of colors from the usual rainbow blended with other hues outside the familiar spectrum. Several bright suns shone in the atmosphere's otherwise vast blackness. Initially, she could not fathom any kind of creature that could live in such a world. For the first time she felt afraid. But the second she felt afraid she was consoled by a sweet voice echoing throughout her body, saying, *Do not be afraid. There is no good and evil here. I am purity. Purity of purpose will lead your way.*

Cistoo could feel the voice echoing continually within her. She felt an inward smoothing, an inner voice saying, *We must continue with your learning. You have an important role to play in the Middle World.*

Cistoo redirected her energy and focus. A vortex lifted her, spinning her into a room where a council of airy, waif-like beings lined up before her. They looked like they were made of smoke. Instinctively she knew that these beings would be guiding her when she returned to her tribe.

Come forward. Cistoo floated forward toward the ghostly figures. The air felt crisp like an autumn day, but it was not cold.

Receive our complete blessing. Cistoo was bathed in light. Dark places in her soul brightened. She experienced an even deeper level of healing than she had experienced on her trip to the Lower World.

The guide you received on the Lower Level will speak to your heart. Our Council of Elders will guide your mind. We will work with your power animal to give you well-harmonized guidance. If you feel that our answers are different, then you will receive further guidance to reconcile the advice.

Thank you. How will I communicate with you?

You will communicate with us as you are now, by visiting the Upper World. Also, you must be ever alert for signs in your environment that we are speaking to you. As you become accustomed to listening to us in this way, you will find it easier to get the message. Practice makes perfect. The entire spirit council smiled, laughing at this last piece of information.

Will I be able to reach you when I need you?

We are always with you. Even when you don't know it, we are always by your side. Eventually we hope to become one with you. Your thoughts and our thoughts will be the same. But that is up to you. It is always our desire.

As it will always be mine. As Cistoo spoke these words, she was drawn back to the ladder and downward to the Middle World.

The stay at the campsite near the river in Arkansas stretched to three peaceful years. No more attacks came from Cistoo's relatives or anyone else. She had learned much from Letodah about the art of being a medicine woman. The proof of her competence surrounded her. She only needed to look at the small tribal community that she had been so instrumental in building. Originally constructed to provide temporary shelters, the lean-tos had been replaced by a circle of thatched-roof mud huts.

A large shelter was built for group meetings when the entire tribe's input was needed. Sometimes the group shelter was used for fun, feasts, and celebration. After a successful hunt or a particularly strong growing season, the space filled with stories and drumming. Sixty people could sit or dance comfortably within it. Log benches surrounded the circle just inside the stick and mud surface. These logs served as benches for council meetings.

Cistoo loved the celebrations. So many stories were told. They gave her a sense of belonging and connectedness to her people.

An auntie once told the tale of Cistoo's determination to play with the boys and best them at their own games. She laughed so hard she fell over onto the ground, especially during the tale about when it had been her turn to prepare the stew for the evening meal.

Auntie said, "Cistoo wanted to run off with the boys so bad that she put sand in the soup instead of seasoning. The stew tasted like mud. I had to spit it out. I could not swallow it. No one could. Several aunties who tried to eat it spit it into the dirt, all at the same time. That silly girl has not gotten the hang of it yet." They still laughed at the images this story called up. This hit-or-miss method of cooking with dreadful results was typical of Cistoo's cooking. Her heart simply wasn't in it.

Now she had a new perspective on everything. The calmness and pride she felt were the polar opposites of the roiling emotions she had experienced when their travel had begun.

At early evening, Cistoo walked into the dense forest near the camp. Little light shone in the woods. She had set out to find a special plant needed to treat an elderly man with irregular breathing problems. Twilight was the best time of day to find the nightshade that could bring the old man some relief. She had watched him suffer for days, wheezing and coughing. His body shuddered.

Daily he had grown weaker before her eyes. He had practically stopped eating altogether. He rarely sat up, but spent his days stretched out on his blanket. He snatched whatever rest he could between coughing fits that wrenched his body and wore him out.

Each traditional method she had tried to cure him had fallen short. The specific plant she looked for was hard to find. Blooming only in the early evening, the flowers were needed to concoct the medicine. She had failed to find a plant in near darkness, so she waited for a full moon to brighten her search. Fortunately, the plant she sought lay less than one hundred feet inside the edge of the forest. Cistoo happily dug them up and put them in her gathering pouch.

When she heard a sound further inside the thick trees, she quickly looked up. *A rabbit, maybe,* she thought, *or a squirrel.*

She finished digging the rest of the needed plants and stood up to leave. The moon broke through the trees into a clearing about thirty feet deeper in the forest. The leaves appeared like black silhouettes against the dark gray sky. She thought she could make out Meduck standing in the clearing. She decided to sneak up on him quietly and scare him, like they had played as children. They had not met or spoken privately in quite a while. He had been such a good friend her whole life.

Almost my husband. She shook her head in disbelief at her good fortune. Her life had taken a much more satisfactory turn. She hoped he felt he was on exactly the path that the Great One had chosen for him.

She couldn't wait to ask him, but suddenly she stopped short. What she saw caused her to draw in her breath and stand as still as a stone. Frozen on the spot, she stood transfixed by the scene in front of her.

She knew that she had no right witnessing this personal moment. Melauki stepped out of the forest. He strode directly over to Meduck. Gently, he caressed the side of Meduck's face with his hand. He stroked his face with what looked like a bird's feather. Then they kissed each other on the mouth in the tenderest way Cistoo had ever seen.

Suddenly, it all made sense to her. "My friends possess the spirits of both male and female." That fact accounted for the couple's uniqueness and for their love of each other.

Cistoo could relate well to this dual spirit. Her devotion to both the male and female aspects of her nature added an extra dimension to everything that she did. She could imagine both killing a deer for the good of the tribe and also feeling the pain of the animal's death. She could express sincere gratitude to the animal's family and to the Great Spirit, but she could also heal wounded animals that she found suffering in the woods.

Chapter 6

The New Arrival

After several years, Letodah felt safe enough with the choice of site to leave on a scouting trip with one of the braves. He wanted to explore other available land in Arkansas. The purpose of their mission was to locate other tribes and resources, such as trading posts, in the area. Cistoo was left in charge of the tribe's medicinal and spiritual needs. In her few years as shaman's apprentice, she had learned always to be ready for surprises.

Just days into Cistoo's role as solo shaman, Melauki, the tribal lookout, brought a white woman to the tribal council. She had been separated from her group as it moved west. Hungry, worn out, and terrified, she had wandered aimlessly for days, unable to find her people. Melauki had treated her roughly, binding her hands together so tightly her wrists bled and dragging her to camp. He shoved her into the area where the peace chief lived.

"Now we must decide whether to allow her to live, Melauki," he said. "I am surprised that you did not kill her on sight. I see no use in letting her survive." Frustrated to be dealing with this woman, the chief condemned Melauki for not swiftly dispatching her to her grave.

Summoned to the chief's hut, Cistoo would advise him on the woman's fate. She brought tobacco with her to aid her forecast. Cistoo felt nothing for this captive. She didn't know her. But she knew she despised white people. She saw them as invaders who had murdered her people, pushing them off the land they had occupied for centuries.

The chief told Cistoo, "We must keep this woman with us, dead or alive. She looks helpless. She couldn't even choose the right direction to find her group. If we let her go, she will probably die. If a bear doesn't get her first, hunger or bad weather will kill her. But having her wander around will put our tribe in danger. She could find other white people and tell them where our tribe is."

Neither Cistoo nor her chief wanted to jeopardize their people. The chief pointed to a satchel the woman clutched tightly in her arms. She had carried it with her despite her long trek and obvious fatigue.

"Open that bag!" the chief instructed Melauki. "I want to know what treasure she holds, that she wouldn't let go of it to lighten her load."

Melauki yanked the satchel from the woman's shoulder, ripped open the top, and dumped the contents on the dirt floor. The Indians recognized a woman's dress when it hit the ground, a mere change of clothing. But the other objects spilling out were unfamiliar to them. They were made of wood or some sort of hide. There were markings on the outside of them. One of the strange objects opened when it fell, displaying layers of cloth or thin, woven leaves. Magically, the leaves did not fall out or fly through the air when the mysterious treasure landed with a thud. They were attached to the side binder by some unknown force. Each leaf had many odd painted markings on it, undecipherable to the chief. He picked it up to examine it.

He did recognize one aspect. "The leaves seem to be sewn to the side piece in the same way that the tribeswomen sew the hides together to make blankets and coats. What possible use can these have?" The chief scowled with disgust at being forced to deal with such a puzzle.

The strange woman felt that she had nothing to lose. She picked up one of her treasures and began to talk. At first, the chief gestured to shut her up, but quickly he fell under the spell of her voice. It had a singsong quality to it like the shaman's chanting to lead a war dance or celebration. The chief thought someone had cast a spell over her.

Visibly shaken, Melauki slapped the treasure from the white woman's hand. It flew across the space and hit one of the posts holding up the hut. "She is working her evil magic on us."

"Wait!" Cistoo held her arm out to prevent Melauki from taking any further brash actions. "I know what these objects are. I have seen them before when Letodah and I visited the white people's trading posts. They call them *buks*."

"Buks?" The chief had rarely felt more confused. "Why do the whites value these buks so highly?"

Cistoo hesitated. She knew a great deal was riding on her answer. The fate of this white woman was a minor concern to her. She had no reason to care about her. But hearing her do that buk talk had moved her in an inexplicable way. She wanted to represent this woman fairly, despite the fact that she was white.

"These buks are a way that the colonists talk to one another. The buks hold information and stories about their ancestors. It is lucky that we caught this woman. The buks she has could carry secret messages to her people further west. I think, under the circumstances, we have no choice. We must keep her alive."

"And why in the sacred name of our ancestors do you think that, Cistoo? It is clear to me that she must die. We must kill her and burn her buks. That way the knowledge they contain cannot reach our enemy."

"I honor your thoughts, Great One, but if we keep her alive, I can have her teach me what is in the buks. She can teach us how to decipher other buks. That way we can stop this communication and intercept future messages. We can know what the colonists are planning. That would give us power to protect ourselves better against the whites, even though our numbers grow smaller."

The chief sat silently for a long while. Finally he spoke. "Your wisdom is beyond your years, Cistoo. Letodah has trained you well. Yes, it is better for now to let the woman live. Go, take her, give her food, and clean her up. Let her sleep. She will need to be in better shape to teach you. Remember," he shook his finger in Cistoo's face, "she will be under your care. You must guard her carefully. She must not escape. I will give you a brave to help you watch her."

Cistoo gathered the buks and returned them to the satchel. She tugged on the woman's elbow to indicate that she should come with her. She followed Cistoo obediently back to her hut. Cistoo pointed for her to sit on the floor. She handed her dried deer meat and a few corncakes. "Here, eat these." She demonstrated how to eat the food.

The otherwise pale, defeated-looking woman attacked the food with the ferocity of a famished bobcat. Such ferocity surprised Cistoo. When she had finished the food, Cistoo offered her more dried deer meat. She ate it with the same fervor as she had devoured the first helping. The white woman had corn mush drying on her face and all over the front of her dress. She was too hungry to be neat about eating.

After that, the woman collapsed, snoring loudly within seconds of hitting the blanket. Cistoo decided to wait until she woke up before attempting to bathe her in the river.

Cistoo sat on the floor of her hut, staring at her new charge. *Life changes so fast. In all my dreams I never expected to have a white woman live with me and teach me how to decipher buks.*

I should not be astonished. Why would I be? Me becoming a shaman was the greatest surprise imaginable. What I saw happening between Meduck and Melauki!

Her mind trailed off. Taking it all in was awe-inspiring. Although seeing the romantic kiss between her two closest friends had surprised her, she was also pleased by it. While she knew that the rest of the tribe would tolerate this relationship, she decided to keep what she had seen to herself. To Cistoo, it looked like *Gvgeyui. Love. Let them love one another in peace. I want them to be happy.*

She felt a slight wistfulness because she knew that a romance was forever beyond her grasp. She had taken a vow of celibacy. Being selected as a shaman was a wondrous gift to her; it meant everything. Her life had been lifted to a level where she could experience gratitude. She would never do anything to jeopardize her destiny. Still at times her body wanted to lie close to a man. She longed to be touched.

Now this white woman lay sleeping in front of her. *Getting this woman to work with me will be a challenge. She will not want to help me. And we speak different languages.*

Cistoo did not fully understand how important learning English would be for her. She had yet to make the connection between the language the woman spoke and the strange painted markings in the buks. She had yet to learn that the language spoken by this foreign woman was in spoken form while the language in the buk was in written form. Even when she would learn this fact, it would be hard for her to fathom, since nothing comparable existed in her own culture.

The female captive slept the rest of the day and throughout the night. She woke up to find Cistoo sitting on the floor, staring at her. Disoriented, the woman instinctively crawled backward and shrieked, "Help!" She had no idea where she was.

Cistoo continued to stare at her. *This woman is going to be a lot of trouble.*

During the evening, while her new charge slept, Cistoo burned tobacco leaves. She wanted to discern the wisdom of keeping the woman around. She had been using both her rational and intuitive mind in recommending to the chief that they let the woman live. But she needed her shamanic training to confirm that decision.

All methods presented the same answer. Cistoo had made the right decision; yet the immediate future seemed daunting.

When the woman awoke the next day, Cistoo looked straight into her eyes. "We will let you live. In return, you will teach me what is in your buks. I know that we each have different tongues. We must learn to understand one another. Then the understanding of the buks can start."

Cistoo pointed to her chest and said her name. "Cistoo. Cistoo."

The lost woman seemed bewildered at first. After Cistoo's fourth attempt to communicate her name, the shaman saw the light dawn in the captive's eyes. She responded by pointing to her own chest. "Jane. My name is Jane."

To Cistoo the woman appeared to be calming down.

"Are you telling me your name because you are going to let me live?" Jane's face contorted in worry.

Cistoo held up the palm of her hand and shushed her. "There is no point in speaking to me in your tongue until we understand each other."

Cistoo handed Jane corn mush and warm herbal drink for her morning meal. Still famished, Jane devoured the food as ravenously as she had the previous night.

After Jane had eaten, Cistoo took her to a small stream trickling from the river so that she could clean her up. Jane had gotten much food on her dress, her hands, and her face. Corn mush hardened on the sashes of her bonnet, which Cistoo removed in order to wash her hair.

With Jane's clear, blue eyes and red ringlets framing her face, she presented an intriguing figure to Cistoo. Her skin was eerily pale. Cistoo had seen this color combination of red hair and blue eyes only twice before, while visiting one of the colonist's trading posts. Jane looked young. *Maybe just a little older than I am. It's hard to tell. With their crinkled faces, all white people look old to me.*

As Cistoo pulled Jane by the arm back to the hut, a pleasant thought came to her. *She can teach me how to decipher the buks, and I can make her cook for me and build the daily fires. She can gather the firewood and tend the garden. I can get rid of all these women's chores.* Cistoo relished this idea. Apparently, the inward smile Cistoo felt also shone on her face. She realized that she was smiling when she saw an awkward grimace reflected back at her from Jane.

"Stop that." Cistoo immediately replaced her smile with a deep frown. Jane's eyes widened as she shrank back in fear.

I do not want to appear too friendly. This Jane woman must stay under my control if I am to get everything I want from her.

Cistoo grabbed one of Jane's buks from her satchel and sat down. She held up the buk with her left hand while emphatically pointing to Jane with her left.

Jane looked confused. Cistoo continued to gesture until she saw a glimmer of understanding on Jane's face. She threw the buk into her new slave's lap. Stunned for a moment, Jane picked up the buk and began to read.

Cistoo had no idea what Jane was saying. *There has to be some kind of connection*, Cistoo thought, *between the painted markings on the pages and the words coming from Jane's mouth.* She sat watching her charge closely and listening even more closely. Then she noticed that Jane turned the leaf over and was looking at a different leaf with similar painted markings on it.

Cistoo sat watching for a long while. After a time, she noticed that she heard some of the same words being repeated over and over. One of those words sounded like *rok*. Cistoo yelled the word out, "Rok."

Startled, Jane stopped reading.

Cistoo shouted the word again, "Rok ... rok."

Bewildered, she stared at Cistoo. Her face communicated how perplexed she felt. "Rak?" she echoed.

"Rok ... rok." Cistoo held up her hands in a gesture, palms out that sent the message "What is this? What does this mean?"

Suddenly Jane understood. She looked around the room. The night's fire had died out, but the stones surrounding the ashes were still in place. Jane leaned over to pick one up.

Thinking that the slave woman was about to slam the rock into her skull, Cistoo grabbed Jane's wrist tightly, squeezing and shaking it until the stone fell forcefully to the ground. Maybe Cistoo needed to rethink the wisdom of letting this woman live. *But she doesn't look dangerous,* she thought.

Jane whimpered. "But rock, rock." Her voice trailed off in fear as she pointed to the stone.

Seconds passed before the significance of Jane's word sank into Cistoo's mind. She picked up the stone herself and held it up in front of Jane. "Rok?"

Jane shook her head up and down emphatically. "Yes. Rock."

Cistoo picked up the book. It had fallen to the ground when Jane had reached over to pick up the rock. She opened it and jabbed her pointed finger at the page. She thrust the book into Jane's face, just below her nose. "Rok, rok." Her finger still pointed to the strange scratching on the page. "Rok."

Jane comprehended her meaning immediately. She took the book and scanned through several leaves before finding the word. "Here it is," she said as she pointed it out. "*Rock.*"

Delighted and mystified, Cistoo pointed to the word and repeated, "Rok."

With a small stick from the fire, Jane wrote the word in the sandy floor of the hut. Cistoo grasped the meaning of the action. She gestured first to the page and then to the book. She made these gestures several times. *This is going to work,* she thought. *I can learn what is in this buk.* Her spirit leaped for joy.

Then another idea occurred to Cistoo. She picked up the rock again, repeating the new name she had learned for this object both in spoken and written words.

First, she repeated the English *rock* once again, and then Cistoo touched her fingertips to her own lips.

"*Nvya*. Rock. *Nvya*." Cistoo held up the rock to Jane.

Jane repeated. "*Nvya*. Rock." She held out her open hand asking with her gesture for Cistoo to give the rock back to her.

"Rock," Jane said in English. "*Nvya*," she added in Cherokee. She pointed to the scratching in the sand and then to the markings in the book. "Rock."

Cistoo rose to her feet to dance around the small hut. She chanted, "Rock—nvya, rock—nvya," lifting the buk into the air. Jane sat quietly in place. "*Nvya*," she said softly to herself.

While Cistoo could not predict how long it would take for her to decipher the buk, she knew that she and Jane had made a good start together. After that first day, at least three hours daily were devoted to using these techniques they had stumbled upon. Jane would read to Cistoo and select a word, and then find an example of it in the environment. Or if it was an action word, Jane would demonstrate what the word meant by actually walking or cooking.

Cistoo was amazed how far they could get with this method. In every instance, she would learn how to say each word and how to recognize it in the scratching Jane made of the letters in the dirt.

To recall how the words appeared in writing, Jane kept a long list on blank pages in the back of the book. She used a feather tip and some black face paint to write the words down. The words took time to dry on the page, but once they did, they did not smudge.

Each day the two reviewed what they had learned. Eventually the list grew so long that Jane broke it down into smaller sections. That way, plenty of time remained for a new lesson in the morning. During each session, Cistoo taught Jane the Cherokee counterpart to the English word Jane had used. Each was learning the other's language.

The more she learned, the more Cistoo could read in the buk. As an added benefit, they could communicate with one another more effectively when they went about their regular routines. They found opportunities in the routines themselves to add new words to their vocabularies. Jane would point to a pot or blanket and say the name "pot" or "blanket." They both learned the names of the ordinary items and tools in this way, like pans, knives, and wood for the fire.

Cistoo enjoyed teaching Jane the cooking words at the same time she taught her how to prepare the morning and evening meals. Cistoo continued the regime of eating only two meals per day. She had practiced this earlier in her life as she trained for the big games against the Choctaws. She missed those times. She yearned for a space in her life when that annual sport could return.

Some drawbacks to the learning methods the two young women used presented themselves. One challenge was the articles in the English language, which had no counterpart in real life: words like *a* and *the*. Jane tried to communicate the reason for these small words. "These words are pointers. They are used to lead the reader to a person, place, or thing in the sentence." Pronouns (*he, she, it, they, and you*) and adverbs (*slowly, narrowly, rapidly, beautifully*) all were difficult to convey.

Part of their daily routine consisted of sitting next to the river shortly after dawn, reviewing words already learned. Cistoo felt pride in learning them and in her new ability to read a few sentences in one of the buks. The pride she felt was akin to the pride she had felt surpassing the skills of the boys or the pride she felt in learning her shamanic lessons from Letodah. She glowed inwardly from ingesting this knowledge.

Cistoo now had a secret she must keep from the chief and the other tribespeople. She had begun to feel a kinship, a deepening connection to Jane. These new feelings surprised her. Growing up, she had had no friends except for Meduck, and no siblings. *She is the sister I always wanted.* It was an exhilarating feeling, yet it gave her great pause. If the chief ever decided that Jane's presence caused more of a danger than a benefit, he would have her killed. Cistoo could not stop him. Another great loss would disrupt her life.

Cistoo watched Jane when Jane was unaware of it. She recognized the sadness in her eyes. *She must have a family that she misses.* Cistoo still carried the pain of those losses from her own childhood.

After months of intense lessons, Cistoo could decipher a few pages from the primer Jane used to teach elementary readers. It was a stroke of good fortune for Cistoo that this primer was one of the books in Jane's satchel. Cistoo was an elementary reader, and she spoke a different language, complicating the lessons a hundredfold.

The chief checked in regularly on their progress. The first time he heard Cistoo decipher words from the buk, first in English, then in Cherokee, he was not impressed.

"How can this gibberish be of any use to our people?"

"But Great One," Cistoo replied, "these words I read now will enable me to decipher papers that the whites circulate. These papers explain their plans toward the Indians. Believing the lies the whites had told them, the Indian has agreed to peace treaties. Then the whites ignore their promises and do the exact opposite, killing our people and pushing us farther into unknown territory. When I am able to decipher at a skilled level, I will read these treaties and know exactly what these whites are up to. We protect our people with this knowledge. We want to do everything possible to keep from being fooled again."

Cistoo argued passionately in favor of the English lessons she was learning from Jane. "Someday I can teach others the lessons I have learned. One day any Cherokee can understand the white's language and read their buks."

"Try to go faster." The chief grumbled. "Continue your training, but I tell you that I will not let this go on with no end in sight. A time will come when I have had enough. I must see results that make sense to me." He left their hut to return to his own.

Cistoo took the chief's orders seriously. "Jane ... time...read." She and Jane planned more study time. Even if they had to sleep less, they would study more.

Letodah had been gone from the camp for a few months. Cistoo hoped that no harm had come to him. She did not worry much, though, because her readings of the tobacco ashes and her journeying both confirmed his safety.

With one brave, he had gone ahead to scout out areas of Arkansas. The point of the expedition was to find a site where the tribe could relocate. Because of the ever-encroaching colonists, they would eventually be forced to move. Even though the tribe's location was isolated and difficult to find, if it were found, it would be an easy target. And their numbers were fewer now than ever before.

When Letodah returned, he had much to report to the chief. "The scouts and I have found two locations that look like good settlements for the tribe. But some of the news I bring is troubling. We camped with several tribes who settled in ahead of us. They do not want more Indians coming west to join them. They want the whites to stop pushing further west to the Indians' new homes. They want the whites to be satisfied taking over Indian land in the east. When Indians keep moving west, the colonists continue to follow us."

Next Letodah visited Cistoo. "I do not like it that this strange woman is living with you. What is this I hear about her teaching you? I am your teacher. Have you not been attacked enough to know better than to trust this woman? We do not know anything about her. She could murder you in your sleep. Why did we not kill her when she was first found?"

"Father, if my reasoning doesn't convince you, please take your own journey to see for yourself how important Jane can be to our people?"

Letodah agreed to conduct his own shamanic journey. He would also read tobacco ashes to consult the spirits about Jane's fate. "But remember, I think this is poor judgment. Neither you or the chief should have ever let this happen."

Letodah had a personal message to share with Cistoo. *I must find the right time to tell her,* he thought. *She will have a big reaction to the news.*

Letodah asked Cistoo to meet him at the peaceful location where he had taught her the original sacred lessons. Cistoo's first thought about this meeting was, *He must be planning to teach me another, more advanced skill. I am ready to learn more. I am always ready to learn whatever Letodah has to teach me.* She felt excited. *Letodah must think I am ready for such a lesson, or he would not be moving forward.* With these thoughts occupying her mind, she met him again at the sacred teaching spot.

The message Letodah had to deliver to her would affect her life greatly. He greeted her warmly but wasted no time in breaking the news. "Your father, Euchella, is sick. A messenger relayed the message to me. The spirits I consulted tell me he will die soon. I thought you needed to know."

Cistoo had not seen her father since leaving their former village. Even so, she felt shocked and sad. "Did he ask for me?" she asked with some hesitation, as if afraid to hear the answer.

"I do not know. I do know he is a stubborn mule. His mind has been soaked with alcohol. I told the messenger to tell Euchella I planned to tell you how sick he is. I also said that you would go to him as soon as you got the news."

"You know me well, Father. I must go to see him. He is my birth father. I owe it to him out of respect, whether he wants to see me or not."

"You know him, Cistoo. He is far too hardheaded to admit any fatherly feelings for you. The fact is, neither of us knows what is in his heart."

Cistoo nodded sadly. "I must go to him."

"I know. We will need a careful plan to keep you safe."

"Yes. You must promise me that Jane will be kept alive in my absence."

"Cistoo, I honor your judgment, but I must know more about why you value this white woman so much. If someone comes looking for her, our tribe could be harmed."

"With her help, I can understand treaties. I can understand the white man's buks. I will be able to read and write. Such knowledge will give us more power in our dealings with the colonists." Cistoo explained to Letodah all she had learned from Jane, all she planned to learn from her in the future, and how important this knowledge was to their people.

Letodah had many questions, which Cistoo satisfied with her answers. However, he still planned to take a shamanic journey to confirm the opinion and to honor her desires, if possible. Cistoo packed a few items for her trip back to see her father—hopefully before he died. She would leave as soon as she received Letodah's solemn vow that he would protect Jane while she was gone.

"You must know, Father, that our chief has had doubts about keeping Jane alive since the beginning. I would have a very difficult decision to make if Jane's safety cannot be guaranteed to me."

"I can only promise you for sure after my journey. Until then, prepare for the trip," Letodah commanded sternly.

Letodah's spirit journey was brief. No sooner had he arrived in the Underworld than he was greeted by his power animal, the mountain lion. Letodah rode on the mountain lion's back to a big gathering place inhabited by ancestral spirits. The mountain lion strode to the center of the circle. A fire spewed brilliant sparks of colored light into the air. Letodah was captivated by the bright colors forming myriad shapes in the sky.

The mountain lion spoke. "Those shapes are important. The woman, Jane, is communicating their meaning to Cistoo. Your tribe will benefit from this understanding. Permit Jane to teach. Some of the tragedy you have suffered because of the whites will diminish. Keep Jane safe. Keep Jane safe."

Letodah thanked the Underworld helper for his clear message. He then traveled back up the passageway into the Middle World.

"The spirits have advised me to keep Jane alive," Letodah told his apprentice. "I promise no one will harm her while I am alive to defend her."

Cistoo talked to Jane as best she could before beginning the long trip to see her father. She had decided to wear the white woman's clothing.

"I agree with that disguise, Cistoo," Jane said. "You can pass for an Indian who has joined the white colonists. This will work even better now that you speak pretty good English."

"Yes," Cistoo said. Then she carefully explained to Jane that she would be leaving for quite a while. She told her the reason. Jane seemed to comprehend what she was saying, yet she looked frightened. Cistoo could see it in her eyes, but she had no choice. She must see her father. It was her duty as his daughter. Also, she saw it as her last chance to reach some level of peace with him. She would never forget it if she allowed herself to miss this chance.

What can I do to make Jane feel safer? "Jane, I have years of teaching and trust with Letodah. I would trust no one else to protect you while I am gone. You have just met him, but you know me. Have I not guarded you well?"

"Yes." Jane nodded meekly.

Even though Cistoo knew she was being honest with Jane, she also knew that Letodah would have no choice but to obey their chief if he decided Jane must die. What she didn't know was that Jane was aware of this fact too.

PART 2

Lokie's Story

Chapter 7

The Musician

At times in this morning light, Hank saw things or thought he saw things that were not really there. On another morning, when he had come early, he thought he saw a goose tangled in the bush; but when he had gone to free it, it was just a plastic bag from the Belo. He reminded himself to talk to Bo again about littering.

The sun barely showed over the mountain when he pulled his truck next to the trailer. It was a shadowy time of day. He could discern trees and figures in the gray light, but the full spectrum of color would not be visible until after the sun's full rising.

As he walked to the work trailer, Hank thought his eyes were deceiving him again. On the west ridge, where the crew had been excavating last week, he made out what could be a silhouette against the pink gray sky—a slim body, maybe—standing on a mound of dirt on the edge of the big hole.

First he thought, *I wonder what that really is.* He doubted his perception even more as the figure turned. It lifted a pipe-like tube from its mouth toward the sky as if making an offering to the emerging sun. Ever practical, he told himself, "Get to work, man." He especially needed to plan this day carefully. The crew had fallen behind schedule.

The Department of Transportation would not smile kindly on further delays. Moving the graveyard had eaten up too much of their schedule already, and it had been a public relations' nightmare. Now that exhuming and tagging the bodies was underway, he hoped the crew would be able to return to a normal routine.

Hank Lucas had left the boardinghouse earlier than usual that morning. His wife, Jenna, was back in Charlotte. Their routine would have to wait until the weekend, when they saw each other again. He couldn't sleep, so he drove to the work site. He could go over the excavation plans and assign the crew their daily duties.

I'll be so relieved when this highway is finished. Traveling the narrow country road to the site bothered him. And it had been one of the more complex jobs of his career. Every time he passed the white clapboard church, he felt guilty. It was a small building, longer than it was wide, with a steeple rising from the top. The windows were opaque. It had been built over a hundred years earlier.

I wish we didn't have to tear it down, he thought. *There are so many small churches along the highway that I can see from the car. Steeples every couple of miles. Dozens of them. This one had the bad luck of having a road built through it.*

Stepping up into the work trailer, he heard the first thin sounds of what might have passed for a primitive flute. He stopped, stepped back onto the ground, and cocked his head. He knew he sometimes saw things at dawn, and now he wondered if he was hearing things too. No, the music was faint but clear and enticing, like the Pied Piper must have sounded as he lured the children away from Hamlin.

And Hank thought he could see the ghostly figure, still barely visible on the horizon. The person looked short. *But wouldn't he seem small anyway, from this distance?*

It's my duty to investigate, he thought. For a moment, he lost sight of the form as he took the shortcut through the trees to the excavation. *I shouldn't have to waste my time doing this,* he thought with resentment.

But when he emerged from the clearing, the sun poked up over the mountains, and he could still see the shape of a person, standing on that mound, playing some sort of pipe. Hank walked closer. He didn't want to disturb the fellow just yet. *If I stay still a little longer,* he thought, *maybe I'll get a clue as to what this mystery guy is doing.* If he moved too quickly, the guy could jump behind the huge dirt pile and get away. Traveling up that mound would take Hank longer than it would take the strange musician to run down the hill.

Hank watched as the man lifted his pipe to the sky and then pointed it down toward the hole. Hank thought the soft, lyrical sound of the pipe was actually quite pretty. But he was impatient by nature. He could no longer maintain his silent investigation. Within seconds, he was bounding up the slope to find out what this interloper was doing there.

But his first instinct had been right. The piper saw him coming, stopped, turned, and escaped down the other side. When Hank arrived at the top, the mystery man and his pipe were too far away to catch. Hank caught sight of him just before he ran into the woods. *He is small, and wiry. Fast runner too.*

"Hey! Hey, you! What do you think you're doing?" The question met only the cool morning breeze. If the piper had heard it, Hank doubted seriously that he would have responded. *Just one of those weird mountain people,* he thought. *Didn't look too odd, though—just a typical pony-tailed farmer in a flannel shirt and jeans.* He saw dozens like him in Marshall whenever he and the crew went into town for lunch.

As Hank walked back down the hill to the trailer, he was in a real quandary. He didn't know what to make of what he had seen. Complicating the matter was that whole public relations issue. Should he call the police? The cops were locals too, and they all loved to stick together.

I can't have people wandering onto the site; I know that. Safety issues. Suppose the trespasser injured himself or someone else? OSHA would have my butt. Hard to say with these hill folks what kind of harm they will do, bullheaded as they are. I need to focus on the highway department, not these townspeople.

Hank knew he had his priorities straight. He knew where his paycheck was coming from. He had to cover the company's back. But he had to admit that he'd be upset too, if he were a townie. Hank stepped into the trailer. At 9:00 a.m. on the dot, he called the main office to report the incident.

"Double your security around that area," the district manager said. "Trespassing can be a big safety issue. We want to avoid any potential liability."

Hank agreed that his crew would redouble its scrutiny in that area. But the police department didn't seem to take him all that seriously. They took his complaint and got off the phone in what seemed to him a curt fashion.

Hank wrote down the day's schedule, finishing in time for the first crewmember's arrival. He still faced a stack of paperwork piled high on his desk, and he felt overwhelmed. The Cherokee were coming later in the morning to discuss moving the bodies to their new resting place, and he had to be there to monitor that process.

There was also the issue of the concrete and of the abutments being lowered into place. *I've got to be 100 percent sure that trespasser didn't do any damage that would compromise our work.* Hank took a few crewmembers to the site to comb over it. They found no harm.

Hank hadn't been sleeping well, so he had been getting up before sunrise. He had nothing better to do with himself. Eleven days had passed, and there were no further sightings of the pipe blower. No more morning serenades. He had to admit to a certain disappointment. That vision had been the most interesting event during his entire stay in Marshall. And, otherwise, he had felt harassed and put upon. Daily, different groups from the town came to protest, carrying signs and shouting at his workers.

"Get out of our town!" a protestor yelled the message printed on his sign. "You're not welcome here. Go back where you came from!" The protestors held these and other signs with similar communications.

Hank had felt his natural sympathy toward them turn to annoyance—and now, often to downright anger. They were standing in the way of him getting his job done. And not only that—they didn't even know what was good for them. He was losing patience with their backwardness.

He wished to be distracted again by the pipe playing. He longed for more clues to the musician's identity. But he had given up on the idea of getting any more information, until Bo Cox's almost offhand remark: "Those people need to give it a rest. Closing up last night, I saw one of them up on the west excavation, playing some hick tune on a pipe. I think I scared him off, though. I yelled at him to get the hell off government property."

Hank was scanning the blueprints, so he almost missed the significance of Bo's comment. "What! You talked to him? You got that close? You are aware we're doubling our security in this area?"

"No, I didn't get close. When push came to shove, he was a coward like the rest of them. Ran off when I yelled at him."

"What time did you see him? Exactly where was he standing? Was that the only time you spotted him? "

Bo couldn't understand why Hank was coming down so hard on him about that particular townie.

Hank determined to wait and hide that night. He'd sneak up on him and catch him off guard. He didn't know what the guy was up to, but he knew it was more than likely that he was up to trouble.

Hank parked his car at the top of the hill and walked quietly down to the trailer with his binoculars. The sun had just set, and he didn't want to be spotted. He sat in the swivel chair in the trailer with the lights off, looking out the window. He swept the area where Bo had told him the piper had last been spotted. Nothing. An hour passed, then two. He started to switch on the radio to relieve the boredom, but resisted the urge. Any sound in the trailer might obscure the sound of the pipe playing.

After the third hour, he had had enough. *This is ridiculous. I've got to get up too early in the morning to hang out here any longer.*

He locked the door behind him and headed back up the hill to the car. As he put the key in the lock, he thought he heard the faint sound of the pipe. At first he thought maybe his imagination was playing tricks on him. So he stood stock-still and listened hard with his whole being.

The moment he was certain, he took off running down the hill. He had left the binoculars back in the trailer, but he couldn't run and look at the same time anyway. He decided to keep running toward the area Bo said he'd seen the guy in earlier. The music grew louder as he approached. Mentally, he prepared himself to crawl softly up the side of the huge dirt mound. He didn't want to scare the guy away this time.

Holding his breath, he crept up the mound. The sweetly playing music lured him upward. Twenty yards from the top, the music stopped. Hank stopped. He didn't want this guy to hear him climbing. He listened. Then he scrambled, frantically climbing to the place the sound was coming from. He wished he'd stayed in the same shape he had been in during high school football.

Breathing hard, he arrived at the summit. There was no more music, and the musician playing it had vanished.

The sheer closeness of the capture made Hank even more determined to catch this guy. He asked some questions around town, but they drew the same blank stare from everyone. Sadly, he had nothing better to do with his evenings. Hanging out with the boys and drinking beer in town got old fast. Truth was, it didn't interest him nearly as much as catching the elusive musician.

This time he was prepared to camp out, to tough it out, to not let his boredom get the better of him. The next day he took his time setting up an inconspicuous campsite some fifty yards, he estimated, from where the music was coming. Because he thought someone might be watching him, he didn't want to stake out his site all at once. *After all, how does the guy know when he can come unnoticed?* Hank suspected the guy had been watching them and knew their schedule.

So, every hour during the day, Hank hauled goods to his site: blankets, binoculars, a thermos, and some food. He'd arrange some brush for cover. He was so careful, his own men missed what he was doing.

He had a good meal at the café just before sundown and again parked his jeep at the bottom of the site. Cautiously, he walked to the place he had readied for waiting. *What has this place done to me?* he thought. *I could be in my comfortable motel room, watching the baseball game.*

It was a warmish spring. Even at night, the temperature stayed in the low sixties. *Although I feel like a crazy stalker, at least, I won't be cold.*

Sundown arrived at 8:06 p.m. Propping a blanket under his chin, Hank watched the spot where the piper had previously appeared. He felt confident. Even if this fellow didn't make his music immediately, Hank would hear him coming up the trail, cracking twigs and leaves and underbrush under his feet. As it turned out, he was wrong. Hours passed, and nothing happened.

He entertained himself thinking about the weekend. How good it would be to see Jenna again. They were trying to start a family, and the thought of being a father excited him. He imagined the games he'd play with his son. Or it might be a girl, and he'd have to gird himself. *Will I want to be too protective of her?* In reality, he hoped that she would be like her mother, independent and wisecracking, and quite capable of standing up for herself. *Boy or girl, I hope our child will be thin like her mother, not portly like her dad.*

He fell into a light sleep, one in which he couldn't tell the difference between his actual surroundings and those in his dream. At first he thought he was in a bar with the boys. An argument arose about who would pay. The bartender remained calm, counseling them in a patient but firm voice, "It don't really matter to me who pays, but somebody has to pony up, because it's closing time, boys!" Hank understood the dream bartender's words, even though it seemed to him that the guy spoke in a different language. In his foggy dream state, Hank wondered how he understood this strange tongue.

Then the fog lifted, and Hank gradually regained awareness of where he was. He was not in his soft bed, and he had not fallen asleep in front of the television. Though Hank was waking up, the bartender was still speaking. Yet this time Hank could not understand the words. He could not be certain, but he thought he was speaking in a different language. The words were muffled as if being spoken into a cup.

"Heelthislaangratespirt."

Hank jerked awake suddenly, chastising himself for falling asleep. Remembering the true nature of his mission, he hoped he hadn't made too much noise.

"Damn." He scrambled for the binoculars and looked toward the spot. He held his breath.

There he was. The mysterious stranger's pipe was in his hand, and his head was down, staring into the hole. All Hank could see was the top of his head. Hank thought the guy was talking, but he couldn't make out any of the actual words. They were spoken in a high-pitched, droning monotone, like the sound of a priest blessing the host during communion.

Wait a minute. Do I also smell sage? He left his stuff on the blanket and carefully crawled around the covering brush. He made his way slowly on his hands and knees toward the sound of speech. The closer he came, the more the words sounded like a foreign language spoken in an even pitch.

Creepy, he thought, but he couldn't stop. He was too invested to back out.

About halfway, Hank's foot hit a branch and cracked it. The stranger stopped talking. Hank could hear him running off. He scrambled up and followed him down the hillside. He had some ground to make up, but this would be a chase the piper would remember for a long time. Hank was determined to give him a run for his money.

It was hard to see. Half full, the moon provided a bit of natural light, but still Hank felt as if he ran on faith alone, following the murky shadow up ahead. He had been right about the intruder's height. The guy appeared young and short, especially for a grown man. He ran fast, but he had a clumsy gait. *Probably not an athlete, but then neither am I anymore. Thank God I gave up smoking for Lent last year,* Hank thought.

Huffing along, Hank couldn't be sure, but he thought he was gaining on him. When they reached a small clearing, the dark figure in front of him darted left.

Thoughts raced through Hank's mind. *If he makes it to that thicket over there, I'll lose him.* He pumped his arms harder, pushing his aching legs to the limit. He was sweating profusely. But luck was on his side, and the guy tripped. He hit the ground hard, sliding on his face and chest. Despite himself, Hank felt bad for him. He caught up and held his shoulders to the ground.

"What are you doing trespassing on government property?" He flipped the guy over to get a better look at his face in the dark. It was smeared with dirt.

"Rape! Rape!" The voice was different than Hank had expected. He couldn't believe what he was hearing. It was a girl's voice. Instantly, he was filled with rage.

"Rape! Rape!" she screamed with what seemed to him to be an unusually ferocious pair of lungs.

"You people are something, aren't you?" Hank said. "First, you act like we're the devil for bringing a road you really need here. And now you're calling me a rapist. Yell all you want. No one will hear you. No one will save you, and no one's going to believe you when I take you to jail."

Hank jerked her up roughly by the elbow until they were both standing. He held her arm tightly. She wasn't going to escape this time. "You and I are going to have a little talk with the sheriff."

She spat in his face. He could barely restrain himself from slapping her.

"Not you, stupid," she snarled and then spat at him again. "Not you by yourself, you and your people, up there!" She turned her head sharply toward the excavation. "The earth. You're raping our ground."

Hank hissed in disgust at her tree-hugger mentality. He pulled her behind him the entire distance to the car. When he had her inside the front seat with the child protective locks safely secured, he saw her more clearly. She couldn't have been more than sixteen years old. She was short and lean, her black hair pulled back in a ponytail. She looked a bit like an Indian with her dark complexion and high cheekbones. She didn't quite look full-blooded in Hank's view.

She glared at him angrily. Her eyes were far set and large. She wore an oversized man's flannel shirt, blue jeans, and mountain boots.

Hank felt disheartened when he brought the girl into the sheriff's office behind him. He felt contrite. He wouldn't have been so rough with her if he'd known she was a young girl. Her face held a stubborn resolve. *This is a girl who will not give in to soft emotions. She is not going to cry.*

"Lokie, what kind of fix have you gotten yourself into now, girl?" The young deputy grinned broadly as he spoke. He remembered the time she had walked in front of the school board building, carrying a sign. The issue then was SAT tests and their cultural unfairness to Native Americans. Then there was the time she had protested casino policies by marching around the gambling spot in Cherokee City. She had carried out both protests alone.

Oh great, Hank thought, *I should've known better than to expect justice from these people.*

Hank spoke with as much authority in his voice as he could muster. "She's been trespassing on government property."

"If that don't take the cake." Now the deputy laughed out loud.

"This may not be a serious matter to you, officer, but I can assure you, it is to me and the highway department I represent." Hank was clearly angry.

"Yes, sir." The deputy forced himself to frown. "You want to press charges, I guess. I'll have to call our magistrate in for you. She'll be back tomorrow—I think she went fishing—and she said I could reach her on the pager if I needed to. It's your call, mister."

"Does that mean she would have to stay here overnight? What about her parents? Won't they be worried?"

"She's been what you would call emancipated for the last year now. Both her parents are dead. She stays at her Grandma Sophie Trublood's house."

"If that's the best you can do, I'll have to be satisfied with it. I'll take her home. I'll pick her up and bring her back in the morning too. I have a few questions I'd like to ask *Lokie.*" Hank sneered as he said her name.

"I don't know about that," the deputy said. "You're pretty upset. She's young. It's my duty to make sure she's treated properly."

"Well then, let's all ride together like one big happy family." Hank did not disguise his sarcasm. "But I want to know what the hell she thinks she's doing on my property!"

The deputy agreed to that arrangement, and the three rode in the squad car to Sophie's house. Even though their destination was no more than seven miles from the township, the ride took nearly a half hour through the winding and circuitous roads. They didn't arrive until after eleven thirty. Sophie was in bed, asleep.

"Look, Mr. Lucas," the deputy said gently and persuasively, "do you really want to wake Miss Sophie up at this time of night? Everybody might be better off sleeping on this one. You know where to find Lokie. I'll take responsibility for her."

Hank was frustrated; he wanted everything settled at once. He wanted assurance that this crazy, irresponsible girl would be kept off his work site permanently.

"Well, sir, what do you think? Like I said, it's your call."

Hank looked at Lokie and at her dark hair, pulled back. The expression on her face had not changed since he had first seen her clearly in his jeep. She glared at him without a hint of remorse in her features.

Spunky, Hank thought. He gave in begrudgingly. "Tomorrow, first light, I'll meet you here."

Hank got up before dawn to pick up Lokie. He had slept fitfully the previous night. When he did sleep, he saw dream images of dirt mounds at the dug-up excavation site, with smaller mounds of dirt where people's relatives were buried. He saw images of Lokie floating above those holes playing her pipe, with low, mellow notes hanging above her in the air.

He got into his pickup to drive to the small shack where Lokie lived with her grandmother, Sophie Trublood. The intensity of his outrage had been muted both by Lokie's youth and by the fact that she was a girl. He had expected a more formidable foe.

Knowing that the public's sympathy would be with her made him angry. *She is one of their own,* he thought ruefully. *She has the same issues that they have; she is against me and the highway department just like the townspeople are against us.*

Hank found his way back to the long dirt road leading to the house. When he arrived at the house, he shook his head. *Whoever heard of a shack with a front porch?* He thought the addition looked pitifully out of place. He knocked on the door, softly at first, in case the old woman was still asleep. He didn't care about disturbing Lokie. She had made her bed, and he intended that she should lie in it. *This morning, she needs to get up and get dressed. This morning she needs to face the charges I'm pressing against her.*

Hank knocked harder. *Damn fool girl can't even get up on time.*

He looked around the yard, and he noticed that Sophie's old, blue Corvair wasn't parked in the back anymore. The third time he banged with his fist. Then he tried the door. It pushed open easily. He stood at the threshold, looking around the small living area, before calling out, "Sophie? Lokie? I'm here."

There was no response.

He began to feel uneasy and highly irritated. His suspicions that he had been ditched were growing stronger by the moment. Since the house contained only two rooms, Hank searched the place in seconds.

He jumped down the three rickety front-porch steps, marched back to his car, and slammed the door behind him. His back tires squealed as he jerked the steering wheel to back down the dirt yard. He drove back toward the sheriff's office.

Don't these folks understand that I have a job to do? There is no getting around it! He felt an increasing sense of frustration as he drove down the winding, dusty path to the main intersection. On the four corners of the hilly intersection sat a drugstore, an ice cream shop, a bookstore, and a clothing store. None of them was a franchise.

Even this main road is narrow and dangerous. These people don't know how to build a regular street.

True, when Hank had first heard the music wafting down to the work trailer on the morning breeze, he had not known what to make of it. After he saw the mysterious pony-tailed person, he had gotten very angry. *I've been civil,* he thought. *I've been cooperative, haven't I? Why couldn't these Marshall people get it through their thick skulls that I am not their enemy?*

When he got to the sheriff's office, he barged through the door. The deputy who had been there the previous evening still manned the desk.

"She's not there," Hank said sternly. "She's not at home. We both heard her say that she would be. You yourself told her to be ready for me to pick her up and bring her in first light this morning. I held up my end of the deal. Where is she?" The veins stood up on his neck. His round, red face reddened even more brightly. The top of his head was shining visibly red through his short haircut. He talked fast, throwing his hands up over his head in a gesture of desperation.

"Calm down, Mr. Lucas. And sit down, please. Slow down and tell me exactly what happened." The deputy's patience rubbed off on Hank enough to influence him to sit down.

Hank recounted the morning's events in a slow, albeit irritated, manner. "Now that you know what happened, deputy, can we please just get going and find that girl—unless you're hiding her somewhere in this police station?" He stared stonily at the deputy. "I don't have time for this."

The deputy ignored the remark. "Since you've gotten yourself so worked up, come with me. We'll go in the squad car. I'll drive."

They rode in silence for a short while.

"Where are we going?" Hank was too antsy to keep quiet.

"Knowing Lokie as I do, I think I have a pretty good notion where she might be." The deputy tried to hide a small smile.

"Really?"

Then Hank realized they were driving directly back to his work site, taking the newly created gravel road up to his trailer.

They spotted her immediately. Usually she stood to play her pipe over the excavation site, but this morning she sat on the edge of the huge hole at the top and played a very mournful melody.

"Well, I'll be damned." Although he wasn't completely surprised by this development, Hank's mouth dropped open. "That girl has a lot of gall."

He leaped out of the car and walked straight and fast toward Lokie. She came to the natural end of the melody and put down the pipe.

"I'm ready to go with you now."

Hank was flabbergasted. "Who do you think you are, young lady? You listen to me. You don't tell me what we're doing." It was then that he noticed a local reporter, Robert Andross, standing in the background, filming the scene with his video camera.

The girl rose slowly and walked at an even slower pace over to the deputy's squad car. The deputy opened the back door for her. He had emerged from the car for this sole purpose. Lokie got into the backseat, where the prisoners always sat.

"Wait a minute, what do you think you're going to do with that film?" Hank shouted at Andross. He was angrier than he had been in years.

"Pretty much whatever I see fit," Andross said calmly before slamming his car door behind him. He started the car and drove away.

With Lokie sitting in the back seat and the deputy and Hank in front, they drove back down the road. Hank fumed about this latest move to generate negative publicity toward the highway department. Then he noticed the direction the squad car veered.

"Wait a minute, what are you doing turning onto Lokie's road? I thought we were taking her in for more questioning."

"You know, Mr. Lucas. I understand your position; I really do. But trespassing in this instance is not punishable by jail time. There will be a hearing, possible fine, and community service. But jail time? No. Is jail time what you really want for this young girl?"

"No." Hank had to admit that putting Lokie behind bars seemed excessive. Besides, he suspected that, for her, incarceration would feel more like a hotel stay. Townspeople would bring her supper and praise her for a job well done. Hank knew that jail time for her would also result in a backlash of bad publicity for his company, since it would make it appear that the company was in the business of making young activists serve time. *After all, there was no real harm done, that we know of.* The highway department would look like an even bigger villain than they were already being portrayed to be. And Hank took it personally. *I represent this company. If the company's evil, then I'm evil too, by association.*

"Okay, okay," Hank said, unable to hide his frustration. "But please keep her off our property. You've got to be more effective than you were this morning."

"You're right. We will see to that. I'll speak with Lokie and her grandmother about this again today. You have my word; she will stay off the property."

While Hank wasn't sure whether he could believe the deputy, his was the only assurance he had at the moment. He didn't want to press the point.

Lokie got out of the car when the deputy opened the door for her. She walked up to sit on her front porch. With a serious expression on her face, she waved good-bye to these two very different men, who each held such power over her life.

Lokie needed to do some serious thinking. Where was this activism taking her? Where would she end up after high school? She had no idea and only one more year of school to figure it out. Stopping the progress of the highway was bringing to her town spoke to her on several levels. She thought about her own progress. *What will I do with my life? I know what I don't want to do. I don't want to end up working in the reservation casino like my parents did. Why would I want to make a living helping the casino rip people off? They're glad to let folks gamble their hard-earned money away. We Indians were exploited; now we've joined up with the white guys to exploit other people. It makes me sick to think about it.*

Progress for Lokie meant moving forward honorably. Not the kind of progress that the white people had forced on her people, displacing them and moving them westward to take over their land. White people had thought that the Indians were uncivilized savages. *Basically backward, like the highway department thinks about our town. Marshall is behind the times compared to the rest of the country, but isn't it up to us to decide how we want to progress?* The thought of the highway department controlling her town's fate infuriated her.

The only certainty in Lokie's sixteen-year-old mind was that she didn't want to be pushed around by someone else's idea of progress.

Would Lokie want to stay in this town after the highway came through? *It will lose so much of its character,* she thought. She wanted her home to stay rural and small. That's what she was used to. But the Social Security payments that her grandmother received from the government for her care ended when she turned eighteen.

She worried about her reputation. *What if I have some sort of conviction on my record? That would hurt me finding jobs, maybe even going to college.* Yet she didn't hold out much hope for college. Who would pay for it? Her grades were good, but she was not at the top of her class.

She was pondering these thoughts about her future and her grandma's future—how long they would be able to stay together—when Sophie drove up in her battered, old Corvair.

"How long you been sitting there?" Sophie asked as she walked up the steps. She had spent the day helping a friend repair her roof.

"Most of the day, Gramma."

"You got a lot on your mind?"

"Gramma, I don't know where I'm going to end up. I don't know what my purpose in life is." She was feeling more confused than ever about her future.

"Well, don't hold it against yourself, sweet one. People *my* age don't know what their purpose in life is. Many people have never even thought about it. At least you're ahead of them."

Chapter 8

Lokie's Day in Court

On the day of Lokie's hearing, the small courtroom was packed. Members of the Church of the Living Vine, high school students, and ordinary townspeople filled all the seats, leaving standing room only. The charges of trespassing and disturbing the peace were misdemeanors, seemingly unworthy of a real trial. Such crimes would not normally create an outcry among citizens anywhere. A case like this would typically not elicit much public interest. Yet quite a crowd had gathered both inside and outside the courthouse.

Protestors outside the courtroom were mostly teenagers from Lokie's high school. Their picket-sign messages were opposed to her stance. A few of them read, "We want Highway 26"; "Highway 26 will bring us into the twenty-first century"; and a more personally directed sign commanded: "If you don't want progress, go back to the reservation."

A four-piece Appalachian band played on the grassy area next to the building. Two men played a fiddle and a banjo. One of the two women played the dulcimer; the other sang and played a small pipe, much like the one Lokie had played over the excavation site. The band was against the highway's arrival. They had composed a song called "The Road's Running over Our Life."

Publicity surrounding Lokie's attempts to draw attention to the gaping hole in the countryside had worked. To Lokie, the highway's intrusion into a lifestyle she greatly valued represented a dangerous change. Once again, an outside force had imposed itself on her people and on her—an outside force that had no earthly business imposing itself on their town. She and her people had survived those outside forces before, but they had not thrived. Whether the intrusion came from colonists, gambling, or the highway, it was all the same to her.

The bailiff loudly announced the judge. "All rise."

After entering the courtroom from the rear, Judge Carnelle climbed the few steps to his seat on the bench. Everyone rose. He had been the judge for the juvenile and domestic relations' court for more than forty years.

Lokie had agreed to be represented by a public defender. At first she thought she would not need an attorney. But the lawyer, Lucy Byron, came forward pro bono. She appeared to understand Lokie's point of view. Byron also didn't look much older than a teenager herself. She had just passed the bar the previous year. To add a few years to her appearance, Byron wore a dark-navy, rather severe-looking suit and pulled her dirty-blonde hair back into a bun.

"The girl is so stubborn," Sophie told the attorney. "She would never agree to be defended by someone who didn't 'get' her."

Now seated, Judge Carnelle spoke to the crowd. "We have a full room today, folks. You will need to be respectful and, above all, quiet, so we can literally hear this case."

He continued. "The law is clear in terms of trespassing on public property, though not as clear on disturbing the peace, which is open to a greater range of interpretation. But I am going to allow some latitude for the sake of both the defendant and the claimant. Each of them has requested an opportunity to speak in this case. As to the charges before us, ample evidence must be put forth to prove their validity. Mr. Langston, as the attorney representing the North Carolina State Highway Department, you may begin."

"Thank you, Your Honor. The court has before it the dates and times Ms. Lokie Trublood was spotted on the highway excavation property. I have witnesses to prove her presence there, which I will call in a moment. First, I would add that what complicates the matter is the fact that Ms. Trublood returned to the site after charges had been placed against her. She had already been warned to stay away. The first witness I will call today will be Mr. Hank Lucas, crew manager of the highway project."

Hank walked to the witness stand in his best dignified manner. He sat down, straightened his tie, and cleared his throat. He looked quite professional in his big man's, off-the-rack suit and shiny shoes. By necessity, he had left the jacket unbuttoned.

"Mr. Lucas, would you describe to the court what you saw and heard at your work site on Wednesday, April 2, as you arrived at work that morning?"

"Yes. At first I thought my ears were playing tricks on me. But then I became certain that I heard some sort of flute playing a melody I didn't recognize. I wasn't sure of the direction it was coming from. But I was curious, so I followed the sound. The music led me to the large excavation hole my crew had dug. Then I saw a person standing on the edge of the hole, lifting what looked like a reed or pipe instrument toward the sky. Then I heard the music more clearly. That was the sound that I had followed."

"Please continue. What happened then?"

"I tried to get closer. I was afraid that the person might fall into the hole and injure himself. But I was angry too, that he was trespassing."

"You have referred to the trespasser as 'himself' and 'he.' Could you not see that the trespasser was a girl?"

Lokie's lawyer, Susan Byron stood. "Your Honor, I object to the categorization of the person Mr. Lucas sighted as a 'trespasser.' That fact has not yet been established."

A few people in the courtroom clapped enthusiastically.

"Silence," Judge Carnelle ordered. "Ms. Byron, while I don't think it is a stretch to call this person Mr. Lucas saw a 'trespasser,' I will sustain your objection as a fact not yet in evidence."

"Thank you, Your Honor." Byron smiled and quickly sat back down.

Rolling his eyes, Langston continued. "To rephrase, Mr. Lucas, were you able at that point to identify the person you observed on the hill that day as Lokie Trublood?"

"No, I was not."

"Thank you. Will you continue to the time when you were able to identify this stranger on state property as Ms. Lokie Trublood?"

"I heard the piping several other times. I tried to get close enough to deal with the person face-to-face, but she got away. I wasn't able to catch up with her to ask questions."

"Would you describe for us the day, time, and manner when you did face this stranger face-to-face?"

Hank described how he had deliberately set up camp to catch this illusive musician. He elaborated on the time and energy he had expended on the capture—time he could not afford to spend away from his real job.

Langston wrapped up his questioning.

Byron stood for the cross-examination. "Mr. Lucas, in the course of catching Lokie Trublood, did you ever use force in bringing her to the sheriff?"

"I suppose you could call it force, but I had to tackle her in order to catch her. I didn't know she was a girl at the time."

"When she did turn over after you had tackled her, you could see clearly then that she was female, could you not?"

"Yes, I could." Hank averted his eyes from Byron.

"So you knew this was a girl, a young girl that you had just tackled? Would you say from that point forward you treated her in a more gentlemanly manner? Once you knew she was a female?"

"Look, she was screaming crazy lies at me about rape. Turns out, she was talking about the land, not herself, but I was still furious. She was the one committing the crime, not me." He added tentatively, "I may have pulled her arm a little too hard when I helped her stand up."

"In fact, you jerked her by her arm, twisted her arms forcefully behind her back, and tied her wrists together with your belt. Are these the facts?"

"Yes." Hank continued to look at the wall instead of the defense attorney standing in front of him.

"Certainly that kind of force wasn't necessary, do you think? Did you really need to hurt Ms. Trublood to keep her from getting away?"

"That flabby, white man couldn't hurt me at all," Lokie said as she stood up contemptuously pointing toward Hank.

The courtroom roared with laughter.

"Young lady, you will be seated. No more disruptions like that, or I will hold you in contempt of court." He pounded the wooden plate with his gavel several times. "Go on, Mr. Lucas. Did you have more to add?"

"I guess I could have been gentler. But I didn't cause her any real harm. I actually feel bad about handling her so roughly."

"Do you want a special award for feeling guilty, Mr. Lucas?"

Judge Carnelle admonished Byron to keep her sarcasm to herself.

"Mr. Lucas, on the three occasions you have described when you tried to catch Ms. Trublood, were there many people in the area within earshot of her playing?"

"No, none at all. From what I gather, I was the only one who heard her two of those times. The only other person who heard her was my foreman."

"Did your foreman complain about this music?"

It was slowly dawning on Hank what Byron was getting at with this line of questioning. "He didn't exactly complain, no, but he was distracted by it. In my opinion, it was a distraction from his work."

Byron continued. "Do you ever play your radio at work, Mr. Lucas?"

"Objection, Your Honor." Langston stated, barely lifting his head. "This is irrelevant."

"I see your point, Mr. Langston. I'll allow it for a few more minutes, Ms. Byron. Be sure this line of questioning connects with this case in some way. Answer the question, Mr. Lucas."

"Yes, sometimes, sure, I listen to the radio. We all do. It helps break up the day," he answered warily.

"Would you say that the music you listen to on the radio, Mr. Lucas, disturbs your peace more than the music Ms. Trublood made playing her pipe?"

"Objection, once again, Your Honor." Langston stood on this, his third objection during Byron's questioning of his primary witness. "Calls for Mr. Lucas to generalize, to offer an opinion he is not qualified to make, and the court is not ready to accept as expert."

"Sustained."

"That's okay. I'm done." Byron returned to her seat, interested in where Mr. Langston's cross-examination would lead.

Langston stood up. "Mr. Lucas, would you confirm for me that when your radio is turned on, you control the process, you decide when it will be turned off and on?"

"Yes, sir, I do—or one of the crew who checks in with me about having it on."

"So then, whether or not your radio is playing, even blasting away, is a choice that you have made?"

"Yes, it is."

"But this pipe playing by Ms. Lokie at the excavation site, you did not approve that, correct?"

"Correct."

"It was imposed on you from an outside, unknown source?"

"Yes."

"Would you have approved Ms. Trublood's pipe playing if she had asked permission?"

"No, I would not."

"And what would have been your reasoning behind that?"

"It simply wasn't safe. Anyone unfamiliar with the excavation site could easily be badly hurt or even killed falling into the hole. The area was clearly marked with No Trespassing signs."

"Thank you. One more question. After you had brought Ms. Trublood to the sheriff's office and pressed charges, were there any other occasions when she showed up at your work site?"

"Yes, there were."

"Would you describe that situation for us now?"

Hank described the frustration he had felt when Lokie had ignored the deputy's orders and left her home early the next morning, returning once more to the work site. This time a photographer, Robert Andross, had videotaped her. She had broken her word to stay put so Hank could pick her up and return her to the police station.

"Thank you, Mr. Lucas."

Murmuring among themselves, the courtroom crowd squirmed. Once again, Judge Carnelle cautioned them to be quiet or risk contempt.

"Ms. Byron, do you have any further questions for Mr. Lucas?"

"Just one, Your Honor. Mr. Lucas, did you, in fact, find the music that Lokie Trublood played to be disturbing?"

Hank paused for a moment before speaking, gathering his thoughts. "To be honest, the music itself was rather soothing, but the fact that it was occurring on my work site without my permission was the disturbing part. This is a huge safety issue."

"Thank you, Mr. Lucas. I have no further questions."

Langston rested his case after calling Bo Cox to confirm Hank's testimony.

Though she had been advised against testifying, Lokie wanted to take the stand. She wanted to give her side of the story. Yet she knew she would struggle to keep from holding her hand in front of her mouth. Every time she spoke in public, she had to overcome the shame she felt about her crooked teeth. Her grandmother had not been able to afford dental care, much less costly braces. Sophie didn't have dental insurance through her job at Walmart.

Byron called Lokie as her first and only witness.

"Miss Trublood, were you aware that you were trespassing on those occasions that you showed up uninvited at the excavation site."

"Yes, I knew I was trespassing."

"Then, why did you do it, knowing you were breaking the law?"

"I wanted to show how important the land is to us. This is America. We believe in civil disobedience if something we believe in is at stake."

"Which of your beliefs were at stake when you showed up on that property?"

"I believe that no one has the right to just come in to take our property and decide they are going to do something else with it. We had no choice in the matter. This is what happened to my people when the colonists took over America."

"So, to sum up, you believe that your activism is allowed because a larger principle is at play here, one of protest against unjust laws."

"Yes."

"Weren't you worried about your safety?"

"No. And I wouldn't sue anyone if I had gotten hurt. I was trying to make a point. People in America get arrested all the time trying to make a point; just go back to the civil rights movement of the sixties."

"So, in your defense, you are saying that you were exercising your right to protest and your right to freedom of speech."

"Yes."

"No more questions, Your Honor."

Mr. Langston rose and came forward to cross-examine the defendant.

"So why did you run when Mr. Lucas came after you, Ms. Trublood?"

"To get away."

The crowd sniggered.

"Let me be clearer. If you were out to make a point, why not make your point in public for all to see? Why sneak around and hide and run when you almost got caught?"

"I didn't see any point in getting arrested if I didn't have to."

"Oh, I see. Your values are important to you as long as they don't get you into trouble."

"I didn't say that. I'm willing to get into trouble. I just wanted to be able to carry out as many protests as possible before someone stopped me. That's why I got the press involved after my arrest. I wanted more people to know about what was happening."

"So, to reiterate, you knew you were trespassing, breaking the law, but you did it anyway."

"Yes."

"No more questions, Your Honor."

The judge said, "Since both Mr. Langston and Ms. Byron have completed their cases, I will adjourn the hearing for the morning. I expect to issue a ruling by later today. Your lawyers will contact both the plaintiff and the defendant when that occurs. Ms. Trublood, stay close by your grandmother until this verdict is issued. You would not want to make this situation worse by trying to run somewhere."

"Yes, sir." Lokie had no intention of trying to escape. She wanted to know how this would come out. Never for a second did she think she had done anything wrong.

Outside the courtroom, Byron excused herself. "I'll pick you up later today after the verdict is in."

Lokie returned with her grandmother to their cabin to await the verdict.

Two hours later, Byron showed up at the cabin to pick the small family up to drive them back to the courthouse.

"That seems really fast. What do you think the judge will say?" Lokie asked.

"I don't know," Byron said. "My best guess is that he has to convict you on the trespassing charges, but the disturbance of the peace part is much harder to predict."

Of course, in all of their minds was concern about what the punishment might be. How could Judge Carnelle dole out a harsh punishment to someone who was still a minor? But they simply didn't know. During the proceedings, Carnelle had held his cards close to his chest. If he favored one side over the other, he didn't show it.

Once again, the courtroom was packed as Lokie, her attorney, and her grandmother entered through the side door. They took their respective seats in the gallery and at the defendant's table. The difference in the atmosphere of the room was marked. The crowd sat quietly.

The bailiff announced Judge Carnelle as he reentered the courtroom to present his verdict. As the judge sat down, he said, "You may all be seated."

Judge Carnelle began. "This was a difficult case for me to decide. I am wholeheartedly supportive of young people speaking their minds in response to unjust events in our society. I can appreciate that Ms. Lokie Trublood is passionate and genuine in her concern for the future of her town and her fellow citizens. That being said, I am a judge whose sworn duty is to uphold the law of the state of North Carolina. As such, I must remind Ms. Trublood that her right to free speech and dissent must fall within the law. A number of legal outlets exist for this kind of protest. Unfortunately, on several occasions, Ms. Trublood, you chose to give voice to your opposition by trespassing on state property without permission. On that count, I must find you guilty and will offer your sentencing momentarily.

"On the charge of disturbing the peace, I do not believe adequate evidence has been presented to uphold that charge. No one actually testified to the fact that his or her peace had been disturbed in any significant fashion.

"As to the sentence, my overall philosophy in sentencing is, first, to make sure the punishment fits the crime and, second, to provide guidance for future actions on the part of the defendant. I believe that, in this instance, an opportunity presents itself to you, Ms. Trublood, to be of service helping to heal the congregation at the Church of the Living Vine. I am ordering you to complete one hundred twenty hours of community service working with that church and the Indians from the Cherokee Reservation in relocating the church and the cemetery to its new location. Since the new highway coming through the town is a done deal, you will assist your fellow townspeople in responding to these challenging events.

"Hopefully, your actions with be a balm for both them and you. You will be assigned an officer of this court who will make arrangements with the church. We have already contacted them. They are willing to comply with this sentence. You will be welcomed and given the opportunity to be of service there."

Judge Carnelle hammered his gavel. "Court adjourned for the day."

On the drive back home, Lokie thought about the sentence. She did not believe that she deserved any punishment. The cause she represented was just; it was the highway department who had trespassed into their town, turning everything topsy-turvy. They had destroyed businesses, changed lives, made churches move their dead. But she was also practical. She knew how the law worked. She had broken the letter of the law, and she had to accept the consequences.

But she hadn't meant to get caught. Even though he was on the wrong side, Hank didn't seem like such a terrible guy to her—just misguided. She felt ambivalent about the punishment she had been given. *I wish I could have helped the church to stay put, but at least I can help move the bodies. I can work with my people in a situation where they are respected.*

She liked that aspect. She also liked the aspect where she would be helping in the healing of the church community. She had thought of herself wholly as a Cherokee growing up. Her grandmother had made sure that she understood her heritage. But the actual time she had spent with her people was scant. Besides spending her very early years on the reservation with her parents, she had not lived on government land since then and rarely visited.

"What is on your mind, little one?" Sophie asked Lokie as they drove down the long mountain road to their cabin.

"I'm scared, Gramma. I hope that our people will welcome my help. They might see me as an outsider. I would have trouble dealing with that."

"I can't say for sure whether the Cherokee will welcome you. But if you go and try to help, I believe it will work out. You will learn more about your heritage."

"I'll do my best to fit in." Just saying those words felt foreign to her.

Chapter 9

Worth Evener

*W*hen this whole highway business began, Pastor Evener had decided that he would keep to his regular office hours, no matter what. He would hang in there until no more parishioners could possibly make the trip. Although he had a fantasy of being flattened out like a carpet on the countryside, he would leave his study only when the bulldozers showed up on the property.

He knew they would be very polite about it. The whole company had been surprisingly polite. In fact, that initial perception of the highway company men as overly polite strangers made him nervous. "They wouldn't have been so nice if they hadn't of wanted something." He knew in his bowels that they were going to want something from him and his people that they would not want to give up. As it turned out, it was worse than that.

Jule Turnbull had been the first to come to him. She had heard a rumor.

"No, no, no, Jule," Worth had reassured her, this church has been here for over one hundred forty years. "Nobody's gonna touch a board on it without us giving the go-ahead."

The church being torn down troubled Jule greatly but not nearly as much as the issue of the church cemetery. Just about everyone in their small congregation had a loved one buried there. Some members had a few generations of loved ones buried there. Twenty years earlier, her own baby boy had passed on. She still came to his grave daily. It helped to talk to him, to imagine him growing up, what he'd look like and be like at three and seven and thirteen.

"He'd be right in the middle of college now, Worth." She looked at her lap as she spoke. "At least that was Ed's and my dream for him. I don't think I can take it if anyone touches that grave besides Ed and me. Kenny already died once. This'd be like him dying all over again."

She and Worth talked about how Jule had nursed Kenny for weeks, watching as his condition declined from measles to encephalitis. There was nothing she could do about it. She had dressed him herself for burial. Dressing him was the last caring thing she could do for her baby. She couldn't abide the thought of anyone else handling him, treating him with disrespect. She didn't want anyone treating him like he was dead, though he most surely was. She wanted to take care, in putting on his clothes, to not pull his arms hard or let his head drop quickly.

Just as she had done the first eighteen months of his life, she carefully pulled the blue sweater over his head. He looked older than eighteen months. Lying there with his eyes shut, he looked healthier than he had any right to.

Worth had looked Jule in the eyes, wanting to tell her that everything would surely be all right, that nothing big was going to change. But inside himself, he felt a hollow insecurity. One of the lessons he'd learned in over forty years of pastoring the congregation was that he couldn't get away with anything. He couldn't fool anyone, not really. False comfort soon showed itself. He'd have to truly believe what he was saying in order to convey it was true. He shook his head as Jule spoke. And they offered a silent prayer together over the church and the graveyard. And over Kenny.

Worth knew that with all the dug-up grief resurfacing, he and his people would need considerable energy to cope with it. He talked to the highway department, but he and his people did not march with torches and placards. With the help of his wife, Lou, and days and weeks of prayer, he simply felt led to guide his church family through the inevitability of the process. They would have to move, but they could at least move in a way that honored their dead.

On Sunday mornings, Worth looked out into the crowded sanctuary. He knew everyone there, not just by name but by story, and not just by story but by being a character in the story. He loved this congregation.

"How could you not love them?" he told his wife. Sure, they were ornery and meddlesome; and there'd been many times he'd rather have fished than listen. But he knew so much about them; he had gone to the bank with Jack Kramer after his tobacco crop failed and consoled Emma Casey when her fiancé hadn't shown up on their wedding day. These were the signs of their bonds to one another. This community was connected to each other in ways no highway department would ever understand—and especially connected in times of celebration and of mourning.

At the Church of the Living Vine, folks had a particularly close connection with the Holy Spirit aspect of the Trinity. The Holy Spirit permeated every facet of their lives. God was a palpable, living presence, not some far-away deity. God had moved in with the people and dwelled on their land with them. The strength of the Spirit could be felt on any given Sunday.

Worth felt the emotions of his congregation. He could tell if his sermon was affecting them. He knew when he was in what he referred to as the God zone. A powerful feeling would wash over him, a feeling of huge energy. In those moments, he had complete confidence that what he had preached was of the divine.

At times, he could even narrow this feeling down to a particular parishioner with a particular problem. His heart would simply go out to him or her. Part of it had to do with the town where they lived and the fact that everybody knew everybody else's business. But there was an added element of knowing he could only ascribe to being led by the Holy Spirit. There were the Father, the Son, and the Holy Spirit, but the Holy Spirit guided in Marshall, like the Shekinah of the Hebrew scriptures led Moses to the Promised Land.

The cemetery had been there longer than the church had. Several dozen graves had occupied the site when Worth began his ministry at the tender age of nineteen. He had begun reluctantly too; he had wanted to go up to Greensboro to study philosophy at the university there. But his daddy had died and his mama had needed him to run the farm for a few years, at least, until his younger brother could take over. He was young, and he figured he could wait, though it made him angry; he felt like he had cut out part of himself by agreeing to stay.

But he always did his chores. He went to church every time the door was open. He respected his parents. The biggest habit he had was doing his duty. It was actually unthinkable to do otherwise.

Forty-three years passed with no Greensboro and no university, but, strangely, he had no regrets. Life had made a decision for him that he would not have made for himself—and one he would not change for a moment. Since he was a religious man, he called that God's will.

The crew's conspicuous arrival had brought home the reality of the new highway. Before that, Worth hadn't gotten a straight answer out of anybody at the county seat or on the state level. All he had succeeded in getting were provocative evasions. "We're looking into the possibility" or "I haven't heard specifically of any plans of that nature" or "Would a new highway be so bad, Worth? It'd bring Marshall into the twentieth century, wouldn't it?"

The idea of hiring the Cherokees had come up at the town hall meeting shortly after Hank's crew arrived in town. Normally, Living Vine had about sixty-five in Sunday morning worship.

But the town meeting after the arrival of the highway crew had packed the house. Young couples with small children, teenagers, grandparents, aunts and uncles, friends of the Living Vine Community, those who had benefited from their benevolence work—they were all there. Worth had to go into the fellowship closet and bring out twenty-five extra folding chairs.

Many spoke in loud, frustrated voices. Jack Kramer was the first to stand at that meeting. "What's this gonna mean for us, Worth? Do they think we're dumb? Do they think we're just gonna lie down without a fight?" Even though Jack was a large man, wearing the same crew cut he'd had since elementary school, his question sounded incredulous and frightened.

With his thin hair slicked back (black mustache equally thin), tall and bony Worth Evener looked like a villain in an old western movie. Once he opened his mouth, though, the gentleness of his speaking voice immediately contradicted the perception his appearance gave to his character. "That's what we're all here to decide, Jack. How best to respond. We will have to sort out together what this means for us."

It had been one of the hardest nights of Worth's life. He had used all his energy to keep from adding his opinion. The congregation's outrage was his outrage; their pain was his pain. He felt his blood pressure rising. His muscles tensed. His jaw pained him greatly from the clenching.

Lou, his wife, had advised him well. "Emotions are running too high, Worth. It's gonna do no good for you to join the yelling and crying out. You need to guide them through this steady. Use your head. It's not like you're just up against Carleton Methodist across town for your share of newspaper space. This is a powerful foe. We need to remember that the Church of the Living Vine is not the only building in town that is being displaced by this highway. Some people are being made to leave their homes and live elsewhere. Businesses with established locations and customers are being made to find new locations.

"Then there are the folks who have lived with all the traffic passing by regularly and loudly right in front of their homes. They'll have a more peaceful existence after the highway moves the road away from them. The transportation department is making logical arguments in favor of the new highway. More trade, more tourism would come to town. Travel between the bigger cities will be much faster; and Marshall will be an easy stop along the way. They think no reasonable person will object to it."

He knew she was right. He wished she were not. He wanted to march over to that construction site, leading an army of families. Everyone would hold up torches in the darkness, demanding their rights, demanding justice, demanding to keep what was already theirs from the beginning.

So in the back of his mind, Lou's caution advised him as he listened to Jack Kramer's question that night. "What are we to do? Are we going to take this lying down without a fight? And, if we fight, how?" Yes, that was the question that Worth pondered almost constantly. *How do I guide in a steady way? How do I do more good than harm? What can this small band of people hope to accomplish against the will of the highway department?* He didn't know. He prayed constantly for guidance.

The men were almost all of one accord. Band together. Present a show of strength. One after another stood to repeat his opinion in his own way and in his own voice.

"I've worshipped here for thirty years like my parents did before me and their parents did before them. It's plain wrong to ask us to leave."

"Edwin and I were married in this place." Polly shook her head slowly and sadly.

The words were different, but the sentiment was the same.

So many people had wanted to speak, Worth had begun the discussion by saying, "Okay, everyone'll get a chance. One at a time. No interrupting. Be respectful."

Hard as it was for him, Worth managed to hold his tongue during the discussion. He reminded himself of James 3:4-6: "Take ships as an example. Although they are so large and are driven by strong winds, they are steered by a very small rudder wherever the pilot wants to go. Likewise, the tongue is a small part of the body, but it makes great boasts. It corrupts the whole person, sets the whole course of his life on fire." So, hard as it was, he listened, holding his passionate feelings about the situation to himself.

A fifteen-year-old parishioner was roundly booed when he jerked out of his seat to shout, "I'd like to see something new come down that road."

After two hours of heated discussion with yelling and opinions flying through the sanctuary, still no decision had been made, no course of action mapped. Worth didn't know how long Sophie Trublood had been standing in the back pew before he noticed her. He had begun the discussion, asking those who wanted to speak to stand, one at a time, so that everyone's opinion could be heard. The men had observed this courtesy for the most part, but with such strong feelings, voices were bound to rise, overlap, and interrupt one another.

Certainly Sophie needed to be recognized. If ever there was a caricature of a mountain woman, Sophie fit the bill. Her black hair, turned mostly gray, was pulled back carelessly into a knot at the nape of her neck. She wore the buckskin dress and shawl of her mother. Sophie had been a heavy teenager, and she'd never cared much about how she looked. She found food to be life's greatest pleasure. She always relished eating it. When the pounds began to pile on, she simply made a decision: she would not censor herself in the area of diet.

Since her top and bottom front teeth were missing, she spoke with air forced between those spaces that had a raspy, hissing quality like a snake might speak if it could. Deep creases made grooves of wrinkles on her face.

"Those boys are tinkering with sacred ground." She spoke with authority. Even though the room had been filled with excited and tangled voices moments earlier, folks quieted down when Sophie talked. Normally, they felt a combination of begrudging respect and fear of her. Some still held to the superstition that she could cast a spell on them if she were of a mind to. But, mostly, they knew how long she'd been around and how much history she carried within her.

She had been at the Church of the Living Vine since she was a young girl. She had never joined; she did not feel the need for baptism. Her tribe had its own rite of passage, linking her to the purposes of the Great Spirit. No further initiation was necessary. Yet she remained a part of the community—a woman who attended all the baptisms, all the weddings and funerals, and even many of the services held in the sanctuary. While she held herself apart from membership, she did not hold herself apart from belonging.

As far as the congregation was concerned, Sophie was neither a Cherokee nor a Baptist. Behind her back, the teenagers called her a Baptokee, or sometimes a Cherokist.

Sophie elaborated on her opinion. "They're gonna win this. They're gonna take our land. Indians know this routine better than anyone." Sophie's voice was full of certainty culled from experience. "They're messing with our sacred ground. We have to take a stand."

Worth knew she was on track, though he did not like to admit it to himself. He had not been ready to state it plainly to his congregation. *Take a stand about what? Just the cemetery?* he thought. *Do you really think that the highway people are going to work around the gravesites but tear down the church?*

Sophie continued. "We need people who understand what makes this ground holy. We need the Cherokee from Cherokee City; they understand the importance of what this earth holds."

"Are you suggesting that the Cherokee can stop the highway department from moving the graves?" Worth felt agitated. "With all due respect, Sophie, I think they have less say in this situation than this congregation has."

"No one can stop the come-heres from moving the relatives out of the cemetery. But the Cherokee know how to move them. The Cherokee know how to treat the dead. I'd skip over trying to change anybody's mind and go ask the Cherokee to move your people."

Worth sighed deeply. He could certainly identify with his native neighbors in feeling displaced from their land.

When Sophie suggested using Indians from the reservation to move the graveyard residents, many folks in the meeting felt the idea was worth considering. A history of close mingling between the congregation and the Cherokee was practically nonexistent; yet they were respectful of one another. Sophie had made a good point about the way the Cherokee would handle the bodies of their loved ones. That was the kind of dignity parishioners wanted for their friends and relatives. After all, they were given only one option: move to another site and make room for the highway.

Quiet had fallen over the hall when Sophie originally made the suggestion. Worth had offered immediate support. He had worked with the community in Cherokee, and he knew about their values and rituals concerning the dead. "Sounds like an idea worth taking into account." He knew that his whole congregation wouldn't go for it at first. He knew exactly who would put up the loudest opposition.

"Wait, just a second. Hold up just a second there." Justin Carver rose to speak, adjusted his suspender strap, and rubbed his hand across his bald head. "Why would we want people who are not our own taking care of our relatives? They didn't know them. They are not a part of our families or our congregation. I don't know why anyone would trust people who can barely take care of theirselves." The Carvers had never approved of Sophie showing up in their congregation.

Sophie remained quiet. She had heard it all before.

Although the majority of the congregation did not agree with Carver, they were reticent to object. Many disliked the Carvers, but they didn't want to create a rift in the church family. The Carvers were obstinate, hardheaded, and rich. It took courage to stand up to them.

"I have an idea," Worth said. "Why don't we invite several crews to come in to talk to us about how they would move our people? They could tell us how much they would charge. And, more important, they could tell us what their spiritual attitude would be toward the job? That way we know what's out there and we can make the best decision."

Carver objected, loudly. "Just as long as you don't include them Cherokees. I vote right now to exclude the Indians. Back when our family had slaves, we did not find them to be reliable at all. They run off even more than the blacks. They don't do much better now in the casino."

"Okay, Justin, we know your view," Worth said in an even tone. "Let's find out what the rest of the folks here think. How many support asking the Cherokee and several other groups to speak to us about how they would move our graves?"

Slightly more than half of the congregation voted yes to Pastor Evener's suggestion. Those who didn't were just too scared to go against the Carvers. The Carvers had clout in the town; they ran the town council. So people were afraid of any repercussions they might suffer.

"Sounds fair enough to me," Sophie said. "I'll talk to my people. If they want to do the job, they'll ask to talk to you, Pastor. They will make their case like the others."

It would have been easy for Sophie to back away and say, "Okay, if that's the way you feel, then we're out of here. We don't need this kind of sentiment. We've already had enough of it to last us generations." But she didn't say that.

Sophie and Worth met and decided on three dates where three separate presentations and interviews would be conducted between the congregation and the candidates for the job. Worth put an item in the local newspaper to call for bids for the work. He got three bids, including one from the Cherokee crew and their engineer. As a precaution against having anyone but the most credible candidate come before the church, he interviewed each group separately before presenting them to the larger crowd. The congregation was aware that he was using this method and approved of it.

The Cherokee were the first group to apply. They presented their design for the new gravesite, their spiritual philosophy, and their cost estimate. Their presentation was thorough and professional. Worth was impressed.

He also saw what the problems might be in the other two presentations he had yet to hear: the only crew who had a spiritual vantage point in respect to the move was the Cherokees.

Besides the Cherokees, the other two bids, while competitive, specifically requested that no particular religious view be attached to their request for involvement. No one wanted to present a religious viewpoint that might alienate potential customers.

Worth presented all the bids to his congregation, and Carver was spitting mad when he stood to speak. "I am glad to see you were sensible enough to have at least one good crew in town up for this job. Like our family, they've been in business here over seventy-five years. They're a known quantity. We're just wasting our money betting on those Indians. I will not put one red cent behind them. Pun intended."

Jule Turnbull spoke in a meek manner. "What I like about the Cherokee crew is that they talked about our ground being holy. They talked about our people being precious souls who should be handled with respect. That's the most important part to me. That's how I want my Kenny treated. How does everyone else feel?"

Murmurings of agreement passed through the membership. "Peace of mind is something mighty hard to come by," Jack Kramer said with a nod.

"Just whose peace of mind do you mean, Jack? The Carvers have supported this church for many decades. That will end today if this vote don't go the right way!"

"Is that a threat, Justin?" Worth said.

"That is exactly what it is, Worth. We haven't gotten where we are without being smart about running things. I speak for my whole family when I say, if you pick the Cherokees, we don't support this church no more."

Worth decided it was time for a vote.

The decision to choose the Cherokees passed by two votes. Really, it was only one vote; the Carvers objected to Sophie being allowed to vote at all, as she was not a real member of the congregation.

"All right, then. I can see where your loyalties lie." The whole row of Carvers got up and left at the same time. "This is not over. You have not heard the last from us."

Several other members of the congregation who had voted against the Cherokee left at the same time.

In the end, however, the majority, though slim, needed the spiritual aspect of the move to be included in the job. They needed it for their peace of mind and for the welfare and dignity of the people they had lost.

The Cherokee would start to work in a week, pending approval from the highway department.

Worth's first meeting with Hank Lucas surprised him. He didn't know exactly what he had expected, but whatever it was, he hadn't gotten it. He guessed he'd expected a certain hardness of heart, maybe just an insensitive nod to his position, but no real listening. Yet Hank had surprised him on both counts.

"Mister, uh, Reverend Evener, I assure you that I don't want to cause any more grief to anyone, and neither does the highway department."

"You seem sincere, but you've got to know you moving in here and putting this highway in gives the lie to that sentiment with most folks."

"Change comes hard, Reverend. I know that. But I believe it's for the best. Even so, we want to do everything we can to make this transition as smooth and painless as possible for you and your congregation."

Worth paused before speaking. *How could this stranger think he knows what's best for our town? He just got here a month ago.*

Then he brought up the subject of the Cherokees. "The congregation voted to ask the Cherokees to move their families' bodies. How do you feel about that, Mr. Lucas? Is that all right with your bosses? Clearly, your people are in the driver's seat. You've got the power to do whatever you want. But, for us, the bottom line is moving our loved ones with as much care and tenderness as can be found. Can you understand that? Can you manage to pull that off for us?"

Hank agreed to try.

Chapter 10

The Cherokee Body Movers

*H*ank Lucas encountered the usual red tape in getting permission for the Cherokee to move the bodies. The highway department officials were extremely reluctant at first. The situation was complicated further by the fact that a young Cherokee woman had been trespassing on their property. Luckily, the court order for Lokie's community service at the gravesites was to come in after the highway department had already granted its permission for the Cherokee to move the graves.

Yet they realized that they wanted to avoid more public relations' problems. When it came to moving the bodies of loved ones, the public's sympathy would undoubtedly be with the parishioners of the Church of the Living Vine.

After some wangling and finagling, Hank talked the officials into it. He had to go through the proper channels, of course, and submit the appropriate paperwork. Then there were the consent forms. Every person in the church community who had a relative buried in that cemetery had to sign a consent form in triplicate for the removal of his or her loved one's body.

Hank would stay on the cemetery site, since his excavation was occurring nearby. The church was to be torn down after all the bodies had been moved. Hank found questions arising in his head that he had not anticipated. *How would I feel if my dad were being moved? Why did we have to pick this particular spot? Couldn't more homework have been done on a different location, a place that wouldn't cause so much controversy? But these questions are pointless. The deed has been done. The spot's been chosen and the work begun. Changing the past is impossible.*

The first day that the Cherokee arrived at the work site to begin digging, Hank found himself surprisingly nervous. He didn't know what to expect. But the truck bringing the five men and three women arrived at dawn on the scheduled day, and they set to work quietly and unobtrusively. They exchanged little more than nods to acknowledge each other's presence. First, the Indian crew performed a ceremony. Over lunch, Hank asked the man who led the group ritual, Johnny Jay, to explain the process to him.

Johnny said, "Before these people can be removed from the ground, thanks must be given to the ground for holding them. The earth would be insulted to have its treasure taken quickly and carelessly. In trusting their relatives to this earth, the families have shown great respect for it. They understood that it is holy ground. Sage is burned to make the air pure before bringing these people up. I call on the Great Spirit and the spirits of the four directions to give the workers reverence so they will treat each person as well as the earth has."

"Your crew is as careful as mine when it comes to digging," Hank said.

Like archaeologists, they sifted through the dirt of the graves. First, the tombstones were removed and stored in a tent set up for that purpose. Some of the markers were over one hundred years old. They were porous and stained with small black spots. The names of the departed were carved deeply into the surface, often in an old cursive style.

Worth came that first day and would be present every day until the job got done. He didn't do much. He hung around. He prayed. He watched. Relatives also visited daily to check on the crew's progress. The crew notified relatives when their loved one was to be exhumed. The relatives who came held the workers in high regard. They were performing a service for them that they would have entrusted to few people. They showed their appreciation by bringing sandwiches and brownies for lunch.

There were 119 gravesites to excavate and as many bodies to exhume. In statistical terms, the breakdown of male to female was 56 percent male, 44 percent female. Of the total number, twenty were children or adolescents when they had passed on. Of the twenty children, twelve were infants who had died before reaching one year old. Some had lived only a few hours.

Johnny had divided the graveyard into quadrants. Decisions had to be made by the crew as to the order in which the graves were to be dug up. "Be extremely cautious to hold the earth together as much as possible around each side," he said. "We want to avoid graves collapsing into each other or under people's feet."

On April 23, the first body was brought to the surface. Everybody was brought up carefully, and each coffin was tagged in several places. Records were kept of each dig.

"May these precious kin never need to be moved again," Worth and Johnny prayed together.

Of the 119 gravesites, all but one had been parishioners of the church. That lone tombstone read, "The Unknown Negro." The unknown Negro male had been a hobo wandering around the train yards in the early 1900s. Tragically, he had been struck by a train and killed. No one knew him, so no one claimed the body. The Church of the Living Vine had given him a final resting place.

Johnny Jay led the Cherokee crew of eight. "Five or six months of painstaking work—that'll get her done," he told Worth.

The first digging was uneventful. The second dug up casket held Cassie Inez Waldrup. Several of Cassie's grandchildren were standing by on the day their grandmother was exhumed. This had been a joint idea between the Cherokee and Worth.

Worth and Johnny held a brief ceremony before the excavation began. Johnny lit sage and smudged the area to clear it of any negativity. "Thank you, Holy Ground, for fulfilling your duty to this woman, Cassie Inez Waldrup. You have held her body, which she no longer uses, and kept it safe from the elements. You have paid great respect."

Johnny continued. "Please forgive us for disturbing you. It is not our choice that we trouble the dead. The highway department has required it. So we do our duty with honor."

Cassie Inez Waldrup's grandson and granddaughter prayed, asking God to extend his peace to granny's next resting spot. Worth echoed that sentiment. "May the peace that passes all understanding be with her now and always."

Almost immediately after Worth uttered this prayer, Carver arrived with the sheriff. It was nine o'clock in the morning. "You can stop your digging now. I have a cease and desist order, and the sheriff to enforce it." His jaws tightened. He waved the document at Hank and Worth.

Carver turned to the Indians instructing them. "Looks like I'm interrupting your plans. You boys can go home now." Clearly the Carvers were not about to forget the perceived insult the church had perpetrated against them. As far as they were concerned, Worth and Sophie had contaminated their otherwise normal and respectable congregation.

The Carver family had withdrawn their membership, but that would not be enough to satisfy their need for retribution. "This situation needs to be corrected at once," Carver said in his usual overbearing manner.

"Let me see that document." Worth reached out to grab it.

Hank stepped forward to prevent any of Carver's orders to be carried out. "Johnny, tell your crew to stay put. Sir, this property belongs to the highway department. We make the decisions about who works on it. On whose authority are you trying to delay this work?"

"My lawyer and our local government trump your authority, son. Especially when it comes to removing my relative from this site. I have a constitutional right to remove her myself. You're not going to set foot on that grave. You will not allow these Indians to get within yards of it."

"We won't touch your grave, Mr. Carver," Hank said. "But you will be hearing from our lawyer today. At the moment you have no authority here."

"You do not know who you're dealing with, young man. I have connections beyond this town. I'll leave now, but you can be sure I'll be back later today. And I will be prepared. What's your name, son?"

"Lucas, Hank Lucas."

"Hank, I would not be feeling too secure in my job right now if I was you." Carver walked off the property.

The sheriff reiterated. "Mr. Carver's gravesite cannot be touched. You understand fellows? Ladies? I would have to arrest all of you if you disturb it. I want to avoid that if I can."

"Keep working," Johnny ordered his crew. "Put yellow tape at least six feet out from the Carver grave. Anyone goes near it is fired. We will delay working on any of the gravesites around it."

The crew did as they were told.

"Oh my God, when it rains it pours." Hank covered his face with his hands. Lokie Trublood was walking up the path toward him, accompanied by her grandmother. "I had forgotten you were supposed to start your community service today."

"That's okay. I don't think much about you either." Lokie said.

Sophie grabbed her granddaughter's arm and mouthed the word *quiet* to her.

Johnny greeted Lokie warmly. "Welcome. I'm glad you're here. We can use your help. Are you familiar with what we're trying to do here?"

"I am," Lokie said. "And the reason behind it."

Johnny smiled. "It's easy for us Indians to feel sorry for these people."

While her skepticism was still intact, Lokie was starting to feel a little more comfortable. "In some ways."

Hanging out with members of her tribe would have its advantages. She felt more understood than usual. "Where do I start?"

"We have two coffins ready to be moved today to the new site. Could you be sure to recheck all of the ID tags on the coffins? We've got to be sure there's no mistake about who's who and who's to be reburied where. I'll be working with you. I'll show you what to do. I'll be your boss and partner during your time here."

Johnny took Lokie around the grounds, explaining the work to her that needed to be done. "You'll visit the new site tomorrow to meet the rest of the Cherokee workers."

Lokie liked the way she was being treated, like another worker, rather than some sort of go-fer. She wanted to be respected, and she was thankful to be treated like a useful member of the crew like anyone else.

"Pastor Evener seems like a nice enough man," Lokie said.

"The Indians on the reservation respect him. He's set up a mission to help our people with their drinking problems. It's kind of irksome, though. The white man gave us the alcohol to begin with. Crazy." While Living Vine parishioners felt benevolent helping the Indians, the white Christians were completely in the dark about the resentment this stirred in their neighbors.

Lokie sensed a kinship developing with Johnny. "The way I see it," she said, "the whites get the Indian addicted and then, after it becomes a big problem, they come in to solve it. And on top of that, they want heaps of gratitude poured on them."

"You got that right!" Johnny laughed. "But Evener is a human being. And we're getting paid. Work is hard to come by these days."

"Yeah, I like Pastor Evener. I can see why my grandma comes to this church."

It was a win-win situation for the Cherokees and the highway department, which was happy to find a third party to take on this onerous task.

"This might sound strange, Lokie, but to me this is a spiritual job." Johnny said. "Digging up people who've been buried for a long time. The Cherokee will do it right. Human beings who have been put to rest should never be disturbed. It upsets nature and the Great Spirit. The human beings have passed to the Galun Lati. They should be allowed to wander in peace."

Midafternoon, Carver returned with the sheriff. "What you've done marking off my grandchild's grave looks adequate. You better be sure you leave it that way until my crew comes back to move her." Carver turned to leave. But when he did he saw Lokie Trublood walking up the hill with Johnny, he said, "Oh my god, what the hell is that girl doing here?" He reached up and straightened his bow tie. "She's been convicted in a court a law. What right do you idiots think she's got to be here?"

"Court order, Mr. Carver," the sheriff said.

"I've known Judge Carnelle since he was a kid. I'm going to have to set him straight. This is outrage on top of outrage. I don't even know where I am anymore. This town's gone completely berserk on me. And make no mistake about it. You will see me tomorrow morning. That girl"—he pointed at Lokie—"will be promptly removed from this site."

Carver mumbled under his breath as he got into his car, "What are they thinking? Have they lost the last little bit of sense God gave 'em?"

Hank said to Johnny, "Just keep her working. We'll see what Carver's got!"

When Carver visited Judge Carnelle, the judge said he couldn't help him. "There are no good legal reasons to remove that young woman from the property. And there are several very good reasons for keeping her there. It gives her a sense of purpose and keeps her out of trouble."

"I could care less about keeping that Indian out of trouble," Carver said. "What about my concerns here? This job will be botched, and then you'll regret your decision."

"At this point, Justin, my hands are tied." Judge Carnelle excused himself. He needed to be present on the bench to hear his afternoon docket.

Carver decided he needed to consult a higher authority—the governor.

A separate crew of Cherokee prepared the graves in advance at the new site to receive the bodies from the old site. Money to buy the new property came from the highway department. They were required by law to purchase the land they had taken by their right according to eminent domain. They used the services of a Cherokee engineer from the reservation to design a plan for the placement. The plan needed to pay homage to the deceased, those who would soon rest in their new home on another mountainside. The local funeral home worked in cooperation with the Indians to move the coffins and their contents to the new site.

The new site was more beautiful than the original one. The new graves would flow down the hillsides on the north side, with mountains guarding them. The middle mountain looked almost black, but the other two were shades of lighter and darker olive. Blue spruce grew abundantly on them. The most spectacular feature of these trees was their color, an almost luminous shade of gray-blue with a subtle green tint.

While they had only worked together for a few days, Lokie felt she had found a friend in Johnny. They talked while they worked, confiding their life stories in one another. Johnny's father had self-destructed on drugs, just like Lokie's. Although he was still alive, he was a constant drag on the family income.

Johnny wanted to turn out better than his dad. "I don't want to put my girlfriend and little girl through what I've gone through. Cleaning up after a father when he throws up all over himself. Making excuses for him to his boss. Getting fired from so many jobs. And Dad's still using drugs and blaming everyone else for his problems. My mom looks twenty years older than she is. She's got nothing to show for sticking by him all this time."

Daddy dying early might not have been such a bad thing after all, Lokie thought, feeling a tiny tinge of guilt.

She remembered the fear she had felt when her grandma came to her to tell her of her father's passing. The expression on her face was really scary. "We've lost your daddy," Sophie had said. At first Lokie thought this meant that he had been misplaced. She had lost her favorite stuffed animal for a week once before her mother finally found it behind the couch, covered with dust bunnies.

"If my father had lived, he would have kept gambling and doing drugs," she told Johnny. "My life would have been harder, especially since my mother died of MS shortly after. We never had much money, but Gramma Sophie gave me what I needed. She's taught me all she knows. Gramma is my role model. She's strong. I've looked up to her since I was little."

Johnny and his small family lived with his mother. "My mom sacrificed her whole life to be sure that my brother and I could stay in school and grow up in the same house. Now it's my turn to take care of her."

Lokie admired how much Johnny cared for his family. She admired the responsibility he assumed for them. He was still young, not yet thirty. He looked even younger with his lean frame and stylish spike haircut.

"I laugh every time I think of you up at that excavation site playing your pipe." Johnny chuckled again just talking about it.

For the first time since they had been working together, Lokie got angry. "Why do you think what I did was so funny?"

"On no, you've got me wrong. It makes me laugh because I like your nerve. Lokie against the Man. Makes me happy."

"Thanks. But it sure didn't get me far."

"Don't say that. You never know what will happen in the long run."

"True."

During removal, one of the caskets presented a problem. A fault lay in the earth just next to the box. Whether from the digging or from a small underground spring, the base of the casket had collapsed further into the earth. Careful excavation was needed to extricate the coffin without splitting the wood. It was in this process that the discovery was made.

Underneath the coffin, which was to be the last one raised that day, Lokie spotted a skeleton lying in the dirt. A piece of old jewelry was wrapped around its neck. Lokie's heart pounded as she lifted the necklace over the skull and brushed the dirt off of it. Miraculously it had not degraded over its years in the ground. In private, she showed it to Johnny.

He thought he knew what it was, but he wasn't sure. "It was a Cherokee tradition to bury a shaman with an amulet like this." He searched further along the base of the grave. "We need to get this extra set of bones out to find out who they belonged to. That requires extra effort. We'll have to mount wood braces on the sides of the hole to keep it from caving in."

The blue turquoise amulet was in the shape of a bird. "This symbol helped the dead pass on to a new life," Johnny said. "The medicine man also used its power to send healing energy to the sick. But I want to find out what the amulet is for sure. We must remove the coffin first, since that's what we were hired to do.

Let's just keep this discovery between us for now. I don't think Hank will let us Indians pursue our own interest on the highway department's time clock."

Johnny and Lokie filled in the grave. They realized that they were doing a patchwork job. The highway project workers would shore that land up later on, to support the road that would be built on it.

Johnny worked on the gravesite himself, in case there were further discoveries to be made. He said again, "We want to keep this just between us. The more people who know the more news of our find is likely to get out."

For the first time in her life, Lokie felt a sense of purpose and mystery, and it stirred her to the core.

Chapter 11

The Reporter

Robert Andross had lived in Marshall for twenty-two years. The photo journalist felt loved and accepted, but he could still never get elected to any public office in the town. A drunkard whose family had lived there for the past two hundred years could easily clobber him in an election. The drunkard would be a shoe-in. Andross would be seen as a latecomer who failed to understand the needs of the community.

And the fact that he dressed like a college professor didn't help his cause, either. His corduroy jacket with leather elbow patches over his blue workman's shirt advertised him as an intellectual type. No one wore such a get-up in Marshall. Townsfolk could see someone coming a mile away dressed like that. The small wire-rimmed glasses he wore only drew attention to how studious he looked.

Andross had come on assignment from Chicago to do a pictorial essay on Appalachian tobacco farmers. The assignment took him three weeks. For most of that time, he'd felt unwelcome. Getting the locals to cooperate with his magazine was like pulling teeth embedded in granite. Then there was Sophie Trublood. He had heard that she was too difficult to approach, so he did so with caution and some trepidation.

Back in 1975, at their first encounter, Sophie sat on her porch, rocking, and smoking her corncob pipe. She looked into the distance as if capturing a vision only she could see.

Sophie greeted him with skepticism. "So you're the one that takes pictures for a livin'?"

"Yes, ma'am." Andross stood there on her porch. Sophie did not invite him to sit down or to come in to chat.

A long silence preceded Andross's first request of her. "I need to ask about the history of the tobacco farms around here. Folks in town said you'd know more about that than anybody."

"Yes." Sophie dragged on her corncob pipe, the smoke lazily twirling around her head. Whatever she stared at in the distance seemed to be gaining in her fascination.

"Maybe this isn't a good time for you," he said impatiently. *Maybe this old lady is senile,* he thought.

"One time's as good as another." Still, she sat and smoked and looked.

She's playing with me. "What are you looking at so intently over there?"

"The mountains. At twilight they change colors: green, then gray, then black. Just because I'm sitting still doesn't mean nothin's changin'."

The spell seemed to break. She turned to look at him. "Now tell me again, what you think I can do for you?" Andross proudly showed her a photograph he had snapped of a farm. It showed an old, weathered house, the front porch replete with rocking chairs, small tables, and a large potato bin. In front of the house sat a log splitter and a rusty swing set; closer to the camera's vantage point were acres of tobacco plants growing. On the left side of the photo, a small family cemetery lay.

"Your picture shows what goes on in most families' lives 'round here. Has been happening for generations now. I can see their whole life in that picture. " Sophie thought for a moment. "Pastor Evener talked about these mountains one Sunday. He called them a thin place. I don't know where he got it from, but he said there's only about three feet or so separating heaven and earth. In some places, especially where the river meets the banks or the mountains seem to touch the clouds, there is a very thin veil between the ordinary and the sacred. At these points it's easy to pass through."

That interview had taken place some twenty years earlier. He and Sophie had gotten to know each other much better over the years. This time he wanted more background information for a magazine article he was trying to sell on Lokie. Lokie's activism had the potential to be a national story. *I wouldn't mind being published at that level again,* Andross thought.

"Sophie, is Lokie home? I'd like to talk to her for the story I'm doing on the highway. I'd like to ask her about the stand she's taking. I hear she's really upset the highway excavation crew." Andross smiled with familiarity.

Sophie gave Andross a stern and chilling look. "Stay here. I'll ask her if she's willing to talk to you."

Most folks are happy to talk to me, the reporter thought, *if only to get what's bothering them off their chests.*

"I'll talk to you," Lokie said shyly as she walked out onto the front porch. Sophie remained in the house, though standing close by so she could intervene to protect her granddaughter, if need be. She would send Andross packing if he upset Lokie.

"What made you do it, Lokie? What about this situation gets you so riled up? Why did you think that playing an instrument over that hole would accomplish anything?" Andross smiled a small, slightly condescending smile.

Lokie felt her initial shyness slip away.

"What do you know about the instrument I play? My grandma taught me to play that pipe. The music it makes is healing. I thought you were helping me. Now I see you don't understand either. Why did you even bother to take that video? Aren't reporters supposed to do their research before interviewing someone?"

"With all due respect, Lokie, this is an interesting story, but it's not the kind of story a reporter would do research for."

"If you're not going to take my actions more serious than that, why should I even bother talking to you? I think you need to do your homework." Lokie started to shut the door.

Who does this sixteen-year-old Indian girl think she is anyway, talking to me like that? I've got forty years of reporting experience. Still, Andross backed off and took another tack.

"Wait a minute. Please ..." His plan to jump-start his stalled career was at stake. He had already interested an editor in Chicago. He had pitched the story as an important turning point in the life of a small town. *This story is worth preserving for future generations living in Marshall too.*

"I'm sorry, Lokie. I don't mean to insult you. This is an important story. You are a key player in it. Many folks in the town have rooted for you. They want to know what gave you the nerve to become such an activist, especially as young as you are."

Lokie uncrossed her arms. "All right, I'll talk to you. But I want to look at your article before you print it. I want to know that you're writing what I say accurate."

Andross agreed.

"Me and my grandma don't have much, but we do have this small plot of land we live on. We know we only get to live on it for a little while, as long as we live. We don't own it, but we're connected to it. We respect it.

"It's the same with the church property and the highway coming through. There's been mutual respect there for years, ever since the church was built. My grandma has been going to that church most of her life. There's a connection between her and the church that is kind of rare, because she's Cherokee. The congregation has their relatives buried on that land. We believe the land is sacred because it is giving itself over to holding ancestors. The highway department doesn't see that connection; it doesn't honor it. In fact, it disrespects it and ignores it."

"Can I quote you on that?"

"You can as long as you let me see what you wrote down first."

"I will. And I'd like to bring a camera crew out here to film where you and your grandma live."

"I don't know. You already filmed me once. That seems like a lot. I'll ask my grandma what she thinks."

"All right. I'll be back this afternoon. I'll call you to find out if she has given permission for the camera crew."

"No, you can't." Lokie shook her head.

"Why not?" Andross was getting peeved again.

"We don't have a phone."

Andross drove back to the newspaper, thinking that the story was turning out to be more worth his time than he had originally thought. *Whatever else, that girl is pretty smart for her age. Very quotable, actually.*

He hoped his city editor would agree. It has been a while since he had written a genuinely decent story that didn't involve an obituary. *On the other hand*, he thought, *this girl is hard to work with. And I have a sense she can be very unpredictable.*

Andross's Chicago editor sounded unconvinced about how big a story this Indian teen-versus-bulldozer piece would be. "After all, Marshall's a small town," he said. "I don't think we'll grab the interest of a whole country. But it is a good human-interest piece. Did you say the Asheville paper picked it up?"

"Yes, Sam. Asheville and the local radio and TV stations. Editorials are popping up. Stories about the new highway's construction coming have absorbed considerable local print space since the first announcement three months ago."

"Sure, Robert, send it along to me. I'll have a look at it. These kinds of items can be quite charming." Andross bristled at the use of the word *charming* to describe his "little" story.

He copied the video and mailed it via express to Sam. He also drove additional copies around to the local TV stations and gave interviews on different radio stations.

A few local teenagers supported Lokie kicking up a fuss about the highway coming through. For some, she was a local hero. Though small in number, these teens posted signs reading, "LOKIE TRUBLOOD FOR TOWN COUNCIL."

For most high-schoolers in town, however, Lokie was some kind of freak. They looked forward to the highway's completion. They looked forward to feeling more connected with the rest of the country in how they dressed and what music they listened to.

Luckily for Lokie, her community service was taking place in the summer, so she wouldn't have to face her classmates daily in school. While she never ran from a conflict, she felt overwhelmed by the hatefulness of many of her classmates.

The student council president had stopped her in the school hallway to confront her one day. "What's the matter with you anyway? Don't you want a mall to open up around here instead of those rinky-dink stores we've got on Main Street? We've got to go to Asheville now to have anything to do on weekends."

"You might try reading," Lokie had said with a sneer.

Lokie knew she would never be popular with her peers. Before the advent of Highway 26, no one except her grandmother paid much attention to her. She was neither popular nor unpopular. She was just there—an Indian girl who lived off the nearby reservation. That fact alone made her an oddity. But other students rarely messed with her. She was seldom bullied. Even when they did, intimidating her was difficult. She was a rebel. She would throw herself into a fight she knew she would lose rather than submit to someone else's will.

As far as Worth Evener was concerned, this whole business was getting blown way out of proportion. This was the Church of the Living Vine's business. *These are our people. Why is the press so interested in us? This is a huge invasion of privacy. I don't get why this story warrants this kind of attention.*

Andross had never been a churchgoer. The two had met before but were only casual acquaintances. But Worth was cordial to him when he showed up for the interview.

"Tell me, Pastor Evener—is that what I call you, Pastor Evener?" he asked.

"Worth will do just fine."

"Okay, and you can call me Robert. Let's get started, shall we?"

Worth said, "Have a seat on my confessional couch. Many a soul has sat on it over the years. I've heard dozens of stories from folks sittin' just where you're sittin'."

"I'm sure you have. And I don't want to waste any of your time with small talk either."

Worth nodded. "I appreciate that."

"First, I feel I should tell you that I'm an agnostic. So please forgive me. I don't know as much as the average person knows about Christianity."

"I talk to people of that mind often," Worth said.

"Good. Okay, to start, Christians have specific burial rituals they follow, correct? I know that there is secularization involved in the burial business because of the funeral industry. Still, your church follows a format at its memorial services, doesn't it? Would you describe a typical funeral you would conduct? Then I want to know how you would square your rituals with the typical way the Cherokee bury their dead. Tell me how you reconcile the two?"

This guy is going to be asking some pretty probing questions, Worth thought. "Until this situation arose with the highway coming through, we had no reason to reconcile the two." He sighed deeply and continued. "The most important element of the Christian burial is the belief that the lost loved one will be reunited with Christ and his heavenly Father after his passin'. This reunion has happened because the departed accepted Jesus as his Lord and Savior durin' his lifetime. The funeral echoes that belief."

"Explain more about that, would you?"

"The funeral homily talks about how grateful the family is that their loved one accepted Jesus. They are comforted to know that even though their relative is gone, she is now in a far better place. The Christian has received her promised reward for leadin' a godly life."

"By 'leading a godly life' you mean following the Golden Rule and the Ten Commandments?"

"Yes, that's surely part of it, but that's not the center of it at all."

"What is at the center of it?"

"The core of it is acceptin' Jesus as your savior, acknowledging that Jesus, as he taught us, is the way, the truth and the life. No one comes to the Father except through him. The funeral itself is more for those people left behind who are grievin'."

Worth continued. "The funeral reassures the family that their relative is in good hands. It's a great comfort to be able to let go out of a person who meant so much to you if you feel they have gone to a better place and that their sufferin' in this life has ended. It would be selfish of grievin' relatives to want to keep the lost one around when they have faith that he is better off. The desire to hold loved ones close is natural, but selfish. True love means lettin' them go, to reach for the prize for which they have lived."

"Tell me about the trappings of the funeral. I've been to many in my lifetime but I'd like to hear it from you."

Worth chuckled. "I doubt you've ever seen the daughter of a moonshiner try to climb into the open coffin with her daddy. Did that sort of thing happen much up in Chicago?"

"Let me assure you, plenty of strange things happen in Chicago." Andross chuckled.

"I believe it. But her daddy had walked the aisle to salvation several months before his death, so he was saved."

"That's something that has always puzzled me about Christianity, Pastor, uh, Worth. No disrespect intended, but it seems skewed and unfair that someone could spend his whole life being a terrible parent, a criminal, and so on and then at the last minute of his life accept Jesus and all is forgiven."

"Yet that is exactly the assurance Christ gives us. In the parable of the vineyard workers, those workers who came to labor at the end of the day received the same payment as those who had toiled all day long."

"Doesn't that make the people who worked all day angry? They had been faithful all along, when theoretically they could have been more relaxed—sinned, if you will—and repented at the last minute. Still, they all end up in the same place? That doesn't seem fair at all."

"Christians rejoice like Christ does on the occasion of any sinner comin' to Christ. Some had the good luck of realizin' the truth earlier, and most likely because of that have led a more serene, less troubled life."

"So then the repentant sinner dies. What elements are always a part of his funeral ritual?"

"'The Lord is my shepherd.' Psalm 23 is a mainstay of any Baptist funeral."

"Even I know that one. 'The Lord is my shepherd, I shall not want.'"

"Yes, with God there's nothin' else to desire. With God, a person has a treasure. And then there is the acknowledgment that the person has had all of their sins forgiven. God forgives everythin'. As Jesus said 'seventy times seven,' which means God has no limits on his compassion and forgiveness.

"Often the scripture relatin' to heaven calls it the Father's house. Jesus said, 'In my Father's house are many mansions; if it were not so, I would have told you. I go to prepare a place for you.' This is a reference to heaven, that there is always a place for those who have turned from sin."

"This is off the subject a bit, Worth, but as a journalist my interest in religion sometimes is more critical than it might be if I were a believer. I've always wondered about the question of the native or the primitive person who has led a good life in a remote area, where Christianity hasn't yet reached—a person who is kind to his neighbors and generous and compassionate but has never heard of Jesus. What happens when that person dies? Does he go to hell for never accepting a Christ he never even knew about?"

"Well, Robert, that's not the first time I've heard that question. There are some who would tell you that the primitive native is doomed to eternal damnation. But I take a different view. I think Jesus is more than just a name and a person. Jesus is a way of life that a person can live by, even if she has never heard of the Bible Jesus, even if she has never called him her Lord and Savior. St. Paul tells us to 'put on the mind of Christ.' A primitive native can do that and live a life of forgiveness and love without ever hearin' Jesus' name."

"You surprise me, Worth. I never thought I'd hear such a ... I don't even know the word I'm searching for ... excuse me if this offends you, but *progressive* point of view from you."

"I guess journalists don't expect Southern preachers from small towns to be broadminded, huh?" Worth smiled.

"You caught me on that one, Worth. But it's a pleasant surprise. What would happen if you shared that sentiment with your congregation?"

"I might be out of a job, or they might just tolerate me. They're used to me. I have some pretty radical ideas, some say. Yet they put up with me."

"So what do you say to people in your church who have made it financially and have a lot of material possessions to show for their work? What do you say when those people point to their faith and the devout lives they've led and say, 'God has rewarded me for my faithfulness'?"

"For one thing, Robert, the Carvers are the only really wealthy people in my congregation. Most members would barely qualify as middle class in most parts of the county, not even considerin' the whole country. Still, you're right, folks do think that way. Folks do blame the poor for bein' poor. To them, God allows the poor to be poor. God has not rewarded the less fortunate with material goods because of their sin, lack of devotion, or simple laziness. Some do think like that."

"What do *you* think, Worth?"

"I think Jesus spent much of his time with the poor. Jesus himself was poor durin' his ministry, dependent on the charity of strangers. Jesus said that it is easier for a camel to pass through the eye of a needle than for a rich man to enter the kingdom of heaven. And he said that where your treasure is, there is your heart also. So it seems clear to me from the scriptures that what Jesus says is that if you value money here on earth, or whatever materials goods you seek, wherever you put your focus, that is where your treasure will be. In the Sermon on the Mount, Jesus says, 'Blessed are the poor, for they will see God.' Maybe one reason for that is that the vision of the poor has not been so distorted or dulled by the temptations of wealth."

"Okay, so first, why do you think the idea of going to hell as a motivation for being religious took hold more than the idea of loving your neighbor and putting on the mind of Christ? Why isn't how you live your life on earth more important than the reward you receive after you die?"

"That's a good question. I have to tell you, I've thought about it myself, especially when an infant dies, or someone who is mentally incapacitated. Do they go to hell? It is pretty darn hard to imagine a lovin' God who would punish someone throughout eternity who is innocent in their heart. I agree with you that the way we live our life in Christ is more important than where we might end up after we die."

"Okay, how would you describe hell then? What would hell look like to you? Is it all fire and brimstone, eternal screaming, and pain?"

"Having never been there, it's hard to say for sure." Worth seemed amused again. He often seemed amused, which surprised Andross. He had expected more intensity and earnest passion about his fundamental beliefs.

"Well, give it a shot anyway. What do you think hell would look like?"

"I surely think we're given glimpses of hell while we're alive. Actually, I think we all go through hell, as the expression notes, at one time or another in our lives. We all suffer. We all feel abandoned down to our bones by God. We're in fear or pain. We lose loved ones. We can't explain it when somethin' terrible happens. Once I had a thought for a few seconds: what would it feel like if I didn't believe in God? And, honestly, for that brief time, I felt completely bereft of God. It's impossible to describe now, but the closest I can come to it is to say that I felt overtaken by an unbearable emptiness, a barrenness like there was absolutely nothin' that mattered. Maybe that's what the Roman Catholic mystics mean when they talk about the dark night of the soul, or havin' your soul dry up."

"You're talking about all those guys who lived out in the desert for years on end?" Andross asked.

"Yes. Those guys." Worth laughed, "but to my point, hell is emphasized in modern Christianity when it shouldn't be. Baptist pastors spend most of their time tryin' to get their flock to take out fire insurance against goin' to hell. But hell wasn't a big concern for Jesus. Jesus wanted to spread the word about the kingdom of God. The kingdom of God is near; the kingdom of God is at hand. Jesus offered a message that, if heeded, would have turned the society of his time upside down. Heck, it would turn our society upside down."

"What do you mean by that, Worth?"

"In Luke, Jesus addresses his apostles by sayin', 'Blessed are you who are poor, for yours is the kingdom of God.' I doubt Wall Street brokers would agree with that. Many folks in mainstream religion adhere to the belief that God wants people to prosper in a financial sense, not necessarily in a spiritual sense. I can't tell you how many times I've heard that from Christians. Jesus did not apologize for speakin' out on behalf of the poor and outcasts. That aspect gets ignored when Christians focus on the prayer of Jabez, for example, believin' that being rich is a sign of God's favor."

Worth paused, and Andross said, "This is a fascinating conversation, but I've already taken up a lot of your time today, and I know you have to tend to your flock. I'd like to get the Cherokee body movers' thoughts on their job. Would you be available to talk more at supper tonight? I'm going to invite some of the other characters in this story. We're sure to have a lively conversation. Then we could talk more about how moving the bodies has influenced the life and faith of this church."

"That sounds like fun." Worth smiled broadly and agreed to meet Andross at seven for more lively discussion.

Andross and Worth had decided that between the two restaurants in town, Fawley's Cafe clearly beat out the barbecue joint for supper. Everyone arrived promptly at Fawley's for the meal. In addition to the journalist and preacher, seated around the table were Sophie and Lokie Trublood, Hank Lucas, Johnny Jay, and the sheriff. Other than Andross, no journalists had been invited. To ensure accuracy, he had agreed that every person in the group could read what had been quoted from them before publication.

True to form, Andross dove immediately got down to business. "First, thanks to all of you for joining me this evening. I know it was short notice. I appreciate your willingness to answer my questions."

Everyone smiled and nodded. Lokie, however, was leery of this reporter who had inserted himself into the middle of her issue.

Worth spoke first. "So how can we help?"

"Okay," Andross said, "I want to get each of your reactions on how this whole process has been for you. Most important to me is in respect to your spiritual lives."

"I've already talked a lot with Robert," Worth said, "so how about someone else goin' first?"

Hank began hesitantly. "I don't think I have a religious perspective on this. I was raised in a household where we went to church on Christmas and Easter, and when somebody died or got married. We weren't a churchgoing family. Still, I believe in God. I try to be a good person, to do what I think is right."

"So do you see God's actions in this situation with the Church of the Living Vine?" Andross asked. "Do you see any spiritual values at work here?"

"Yes. Believe it or not, I have thought about this. I expected people to be meaner and harder to get along with. I knew I was coming in and asking a lot of folks to move from a place they loved to somewhere else. I knew that would be hard for them. But I believe in what I do. I believe in bringing progress to places like this. It changes people's lives for the better. I think God would approve of that."

Lokie squirmed in her chair. "How do you know what God thinks is progress?"

Hank felt his face warming, and a tinge of sarcasm crept into his voice. "My own experience—which, by the way, is huge in this area."

Lokie continued. "What does your *huge* experience tell you?"

"My experience tells me that people are happier after a new highway comes into their town. It's easier to get to other towns. People will be more connected to the outside world. They'll have better access to the latest technology.

"Trucks can get to where they're going faster, bringing new products with them. Tourists will come to town and spend money. The town will be wealthier overall. All of that's good, in my humble opinion. So if peoples' lives are better, why wouldn't God approve of that?"

"The town would become wealthier, you said? My grandma taught me that Jesus was a great shaman who didn't care at all about getting rich. That's not our number-one concern in Marshall either. The argument that you make is the same argument that the Cherokee have been hearing since the whites hit the coast of our country. The colonists thought, *We'll bring progress to these savages. They don't know how to read or write. They run around with their clothes off. They build weird-looking homes. They love to kill each other. They don't know how to grow crops. Yeah, we have to teach these primitives.* All along, what they really wanted was to push us further west and take our land, all in the name of progress."

"I don't think you can compare what happened a couple of hundred years ago to what's happening now, Ms. Trublood." Hank's politeness seemed phony to her. "Roads support business in our country. History has proven that."

"Yes, if you believe in capitalism. Your argument doesn't include the good parts of Cherokee lives before the colonists got here."

"Just get over it, Lokie. That was then. This is now. America has become the greatest nation in the world. There had to be some sacrifices along the way to achieve that status."

"Easy for you to say, *Hank*, when the sacrifices were not on the backs of your people."

"I think we're movin' away from Robert's question, Hank," Worth said. "I know everyone speakin' cares about what they're sayin.' Let's try to take a closer look at Robert's actual question. Has this highway comin' through had a spiritual effect on our community, for good or bad?"

Johnny spoke next. "Well, I see that it has brought our people a little closer with the townspeople. Before the highway, we got along but were not what you'd call friendly with one another. We would have our disagreements, and someone, usually the Indian, would end up losing. I think our relations with the church are better. We respect each other more. The Cherokee appreciate the care the church wants to take in handling their relatives. The congregation appreciates the care that the Cherokee are taking in moving those people. A few holdouts wouldn't let go of their prejudices if their lives depended on it, but in all I think the relations between the Indians and the church people are more balanced."

"Yes, balance is key for the Indian," Sophie added. "It is the aim of the Cherokee Nation to maintain balance between the Upper World, *Galvladitlv Elohi,* and the *Eladige Elohi,* the Lower World. This seems to be a situation where balance is tipping in favor of better relations. The Great One would like that."

Lokie sneered. "I wonder if the Great One is pleased by the progress the Cherokee have made on the reservation. Most Indians earn their living by robbing other folks in the white man's casino. But the white owners keep most of the money."

"You've changed the subject, Lokie, and you are not answering the question Mr. Andross asked," Worth said gently.

"All I'm saying is, I don't see anything spiritual about what white people think of as progress."

"Do you think you being so mad about this *white man's progress* gives you the right to break the law?" Hank blurted out. "That's what you were doing when you trespassed on government property. You've caused quite a stir that doesn't help anybody. Do you think that your Great One is pleased with you just now?"

"You're so above us, aren't you?" Lokie yelled.

Other customers in the café turned to check out the ruckus. And luckily the meals came. Both the aromas of the home cooking and the desire to seem dignified in front of the waiter chastened Lokie and Hank for the moment, as the platters were placed before each person.

Worth said grace: "Bless this food which we are about to receive. We thank the server who brought it, the cooks who prepared it, and the plants and animals who gave themselves so that we might be nourished. In Jesus' name, we pray. Amen."

"I wonder if we could continue this discussion without insulting each other," Andross said. "As a journalist, I know that it's possible to get your points across without resorting to the use of rhetoric or sarcasm."

A hush fell over the table as everyone ate and gathered their thoughts. Lokie wasn't sure what *rhetoric* meant, but she knew she was one of the people Andross was addressing.

Lokie noticed Andross dig into his food with abandon. *I guess he's worked up quite an appetite listening to us argue.*

The restaurant manager stopped to visit the table and to check on the service. "I hope you're enjoying the food." He started to leave but turned back around, looked at Lokie, and gushed, "I really admire the stand you've taken about the new highway."

Hank immediately jumped in. "Don't forget. You'll get more customers when tourists come through. You're being shortsighted."

The restaurant manager swallowed hard while remaining patient. "Mister ...?"

"Hank Lucas."

"Mr. Lucas, we're a local restaurant with a local clientele. We've been happy with that situation since we opened in 1983. We don't need any more customers. We support our family just fine."

Hank shook his head and looked down at his plate.

"Well, enjoy." The owner returned to the kitchen. Despite it being a Wednesday night, the dining room was full of customers. They had flocked in for the blue-plate special—a hot turkey sandwich on a homemade roll with mashed potatoes and gravy, served with fresh cranberry sauce.

"So, Mr. Jay," Andross turned to the reburial crew leader. "What do you see in Indian spirituality that is different from Pastor Evener's situation at his church?"

"The difference is our beliefs. The Cherokee care about how the human beings buried in those graves are treated. We understand that they should never have to be moved. Disturbing the land and the ancestors is wrong. It must be taken serious. It is an Indian custom that mistreatment of the dead brings sickness to the living. That may sound crazy to Christians, but it's a belief our people still hold."

Worth elaborated on his opinion. "I've seen a real change in our congregation since the decision was made to stop fightin' the highway department. We decided to move our church and our people forward. At first, most everyone was up in arms, determined to stay put. But we quickly learned that would not work. So we swallowed our grief and got down to business. Here I have to thank Sophie Trublood for bringin' up the idea of havin' the Cherokee move the bodies."

"That wasn't totally an easy sell, was it, Worth?" Sophie showed her toothless grin.

"No, but the majority of the congregation eventually went along. After folks saw the work your people do, most doubt about the process disappeared."

"It's like seein' the sun shinin' behind a dark cloud. I think this is a situation where it has been important to have faith in God's future for us. Like the Bible says, being anxious about your life isn't a good idea; tryin' to avoid an unpleasant outcome isn't always possible. You have to let go and let God. Then there's room for an unexpected surprise, somethin' that no one had anticipated.

"In this case, it's the Cherokee movin' the bodies, which connects the whites and the Indians in a way they had not been connected before. And the word spreads that the Cherokee can be counted on to help a congregation in a time of great need with great gentleness and sensitivity. I see God's action in that."

The moment Worth finished speaking, Carver and his assistant burst into the restaurant and rudely broke into the group's conversation. He had brought another piece of official paperwork with him. "You, young lady, are fired. You're off the job. The governor has signed my request for removin' you from the gravesite."

Lokie was shocked. "What? You can't do that!"

"I most certainly can. And all your objections will get you absolutely nothin'."

"And what is the reason behind that decision?" Worth asked.

"As an attorney, the governor agrees with me. It's a conflict of interest for someone with a known antagonism toward the highway department to work on a project linked to them. Hell, she got convicted of a crime against them."

"That's hogwash." Johnny stood up, his face contorted with anger.

Andross, who always carried his camera with him, shot several pictures of Carver's advance to the table as well as his serving the paper officially banishing Lokie from the job.

Andross's best shot was of Carver leaning forward toward Lokie, his finger pointed in her face. In his other hand, he lifted over his head the letter from the governor dismissing Lokie.

Carver turned to Worth. "You may have a new church comin' up on a new mountain, but I'm taking a good twenty members with me. We're joinin' Alton Baptist, and all our tithes will be goin' there. You should have listened to us before pickin' this Indian crew. And, you, Mr. Andross, if you use my picture in print or write about me without my permission, I will sue you for libel!"

Carver and his associate slammed the door behind them as they left the restaurant.

Chapter 12

The Storyteller

After the unceremonious end to their meal at Fawley's, Johnny and Lokie went to Dairy Queen to talk privately about her getting fired.

"It's a bummer I'm not going to get to work at the site with you anymore, Johnny, but maybe this is our chance to find out more about our discovery."

"That's true, but I don't know what to do next?"

"I'll bet Mr. Andross has contacts with forensic scientists. As a reporter, he's had to have spent a lot of time talking to police and their crime labs."

"I don't know if I want to let another person in on this, especially not somebody who reports news to the public."

"You've got a point, Johnny." Lokie paused for a moment to think. "We owe it to our tribe's history to find out who these bones belong to and exactly what this amulet means. Maybe there's a way we can get Andross to help without telling him everything we've got."

"Just hold up a minute, Lokie. You know, I'm worried. I don't want the church to think we're double-crossing them. The people respect us more now. I don't want them to see us as thieves."

"For one thing, we should have had their respect all along. For another thing, we have lots of reason to disrespect them—"

Lokie stopped in midsentence. She had told herself beforehand not to be preachy. After all, she was talking to someone who agreed with her. And she didn't want to be annoying. She wanted to make a logical case.

Johnny agreed with Lokie's reasoning.

Andross agreed to contact one of his good friends in Raleigh at the police department there. "Dr. Lindstrom has worked many cases; his specialty is determining a crime victim's identity from examining his skeletal remains. I'll do this for you. But you've got to let me in on the story after you get the answers you're looking for."

Johnny took a day off from work at the site. He and Lokie rode to Raleigh together to meet Dr. Lindstrom.

"These remains are in rough shape," Lindstrom said. "Been in the ground a good while, I'd say. But I'm going to figure out who belonged to them. Trust me; I'll bring his identity to light— and learn something in the process, I'm sure.

"The skeleton is too old and too long in the ground. But I can tell you characteristics of the person who hung on this frame. It'll take a day or two. I'll get back to you. This is a fun mystery for me to unravel—different from the typical grizzly crime I work on. I'm glad Andross sent you to me."

"Oh, believe me, we are grateful to you," Johnny said. "We believe your findings can help fill in some gaps in our Cherokee history."

"So let's get started. I'll have to move these objects to a sterile environment. I'll perform a series of tests on them and keep you up to date on my findings."

Dr. Lindstrom took the skeleton to the forensic laboratory, where the bones would be analyzed. After three days of analysis in addition to doing his actual job, Lindstrom called Johnny and Lokie with the results. "I can tell you that these bones belong to a Native American male in his mid forties. The wide brow is a chief characteristic in making that determination. He died from an apparent upper respiratory problem—TB, perhaps, or pneumonia. I've dated the bones back to the early eighteen hundreds, 1810–1820, approximately. Signs of damage within the bone marrow suggest excessive alcohol consumption. Judging from the place where you found him and the time period, I would say he was a member of the western North Carolina Cherokee tribe of that era. He must have spent part of his life as a warrior or hunter, because the bones show injuries congruent with those from arrows or some kind of spear."

Johnny was amazed. "That is a lot of information."

"The curious thing is what you told me about finding the amulet of a shaman around his neck. That doesn't seem to fit with this man, who must have stayed drunk for most of his adult life. I say that because of the damage done to his marrow."

"Are you saying that the necklace and the body don't seem to go together?" Lokie asked.

"Yes, but he could've just been a bad shaman. My suggestion is that you look into the history of tribes in the area during that period. I would look more into oral history."

"We'd have to use oral history," Lokie said. "There wasn't anything written down until after Sequoyah invented the alphabet. That was about 1824. All us Indian kids learned that in grade school."

"Then oral tradition is the best way for you to go."

"At least we have more to go on in pursuing our detective work," Johnny said.

When he and Lokie visited the library at Duke, they found a photograph in a book of Indian art circa 1800 showing drawings of various shamans' amulets. One, in particular, resembled the one they had found. The amulet was a typical medicine man's ornament of the Cherokee tribe in West Carolina and environs.

Book notes stated that these amulets were thought to have "specific healing properties of their own." Further notes said,

"The amulet's healing power also extended to its ability to lead the dead and dying peacefully into the next world."

When she got home, Lokie found a subpoena on her door to appear in court the next day. "What's this all about, Gramma?"

"A deputy came by while you were gone. You've got to go back before Judge Carnelle. He has to give you a new assignment, since the Carvers got you kicked off the last one. You're supposed to go tomorrow. I'll drive you there."

Lokie was more concerned about what she and Johnny had learned in Raleigh and at the Duke Library. As usual, she shared it all with her grandmother. And Sophie had a suggestion of her own. "I stay in touch with the Barefoot family. The old woman in their family is close to a hundred years old."

Sophie called the family to arrange a meeting with Lokie and Johnny. At their first get-together Lokie explained to the Barefoot couple the nature of the discovery at the church burial site. She helped them to understand the reason she thought their family could help with this project. "Do you think that your great aunt is up for an interview or two?" Lokie asked.

"Of course we will have to ask her." The two exchanged knowing glances.

The granddaughter continued. "She is sharp as a tack at ninety-seven. And she's going to love sharing what she knows. She's a great storyteller, but she doesn't get much chance to share them like she used to. Her grandchildren have heard them all before, and the great grandchildren are teenagers. You know teenagers." She blushed slightly realizing that they were talking to one. "Sorry."

"No offense taken. They're busy with their own lives, I guess," Lokie said.

"Yes, different than you, actually. My guess is Auntie Jess will be very happy to talk with you. She'll enjoy the company. But we'll call you after we get the go-ahead from her."

At this point, Johnny and Lokie decided to tell Worth about the discovery.

"I'm disappointed you didn't tell me earlier," Worth said. "I wouldn't have minded you pursuing it. What the congregation would think is a different matter. Explaining it to them now might be hard, especially with Carver's continuing harassment. But it is my duty to tell them about it. You see that, don't you?"

Both Johnny and Lokie agreed, but Lokie was afraid that it would backfire against both of them.

The visit to Judge Carnelle with Sophie was not productive.

"I will have to give your next community service a great deal of thought, Lokie," he said. "Working at the church cemetery seemed like such a good opportunity for you and the church. Let's talk again soon, after I've had more time to consider what I'm going to do next."

"Would you be willing to allow me to do research as community service? On behalf of my people's history?" Lokie asked.

Judge Carnelle furrowed his brow, as if puzzled. "I don't know, Lokie. That seems highly unusual. I'll have to get back to you on that. Come back next week for my decision."

Lokie, Johnny, Worth, Andross, and Sophie all went to visit Jess Barefoot, the storyteller. She had baked two pies, pecan and lemon meringue, in their honor. Sophie had grown up listening to Jess's stories. Lokie wished that her grandmother remembered more of what she had heard as a child.

Jess had been born on the reservation in 1900. She came from a long line of storytellers, or "keepers of the families' history," as she liked to say.

"Welcome to my home," she said as she pointed to the scant seating in her living room. Lokie and Johnny sat on the floor. Her house was small but neat. Out back was a vegetable garden Jess still tended. On the wall hung a handmade quilt she had completed with her Cherokee quilting group. The pattern was one of stylized designs of bears and birds.

Jess was a tiny, wizened woman. She had lost most of her hair over the years; a single, white patch sprouted comically from the top of her head. Her hands were very animated as she spoke. "What can I tell you young people today? I figured we could talk for a while, then have some pie. Then maybe we could talk some more. Living alone, I don't visit with folks often. It's my pure pleasure to see you."

Clearly Jess is in full possession of her faculties, Lokie thought. *Chatty to boot.*

Lokie began the conversation with a question: "Do you have any stories from the early part of the 1800s?"

"Oh yes, too many to repeat them all in one day. Lots of stories back to my great grandmother and before. She never got tired of telling me stories." Jess laughed heartily, her shoulders bobbing up and down as she did. The wisp of a woman had a big laugh. It sounded as if it had erupted from the belly of a more sizeable creature.

"Sometimes I wished she would have just been quiet and brushed my hair or talked to me about ordinary things. But she knew it was her job to keep the families' stories alive."

"Is that how you feel, Miss Jess? About keeping the stories alive?" Lokie asked.

"You bet I do! Without folks like me, outsiders would not know what really happened. I am a keeper of the truth—a keeper of the families' stories and a keeper of the truth.'"

"But how can you be sure that you're tellin' the same story that was told to you?" Worth asked. "I can see how the stories might get changed over time—like they do in that children's game called Gossip."

"I'm glad you asked that, Pastor. I think some people are just wrongheaded about how the history is passed down. More care is given than you might think. It's like reading the same bedtime story to your child over and over. Pretty soon they're reading it along with you word for word. Well, just like the words in the book don't change, the words in the stories passed on don't change. We hear the exact same stories told many times over in the same words. My grandmother learned the stories that way, and that's how I learned them."

"You mean you had to memorize these stories exactly as you heard them?" Lokie was amazed.

"Yes. When I was chosen to be a storyteller, my job was to retell the story exactly like I heard it. It was a sacred job. My grandmother made me repeat the stories back to her many times. If I got even one word wrong, I had to start over. So I listened to these stories over and over. I told them again and again. You bet I knew them word for word. They came out of me naturally.

"So they were burnt into my memory. I couldn't have forgotten them if I tried. Even the way my grandmother told the stories—the stops and starts, the ups and downs, her putting more weight on some parts than others. I took all that in too. If it was possible to put both of us side by side and have us tell the story at the same time, we would be talking in stereo." Jess laughed at the wonder of it.

"We are interested in what you might know about this amulet." Lokie showed her the necklace. "Your great-grandmother would have been little when this happened. Alcoholism and shamanism are other details of the story we are looking into."

"Oh yes, I know this amulet. I've never seen one in person, but my ancestors have described them to me. Shamans wore them."

With Miss Jess's permission, Andross began to tape the conversation.

"Was a shaman usually buried wearing his amulet?" Lokie asked.

"No. When a shaman died, the amulet passed down to his apprentice. The next shaman passed the amulet down to his apprentice and so on and so on."

"That's interesting," Johnny said. "So the fact that we found the amulet around the neck of the skeleton does not automatically mean that the body belonged to a shaman?"

"No, no. What you describe is very unusual." Jess paused. Her face reflected the dawning of a forgotten memory. "Actually, it reminds me of something—not a story passed down to me but an interesting tale anyway."

"Oh, please tell us!" Lokie said.

"Sure. Part of our oral tradition connects to a woman shaman named Cistoo. She was a strong girl, a swift runner and deadeye hunter. Eventually, she was honored as a great shaman by all the Cherokee. It is thought that she and her captive, Jane, helped Sequoyah develop our alphabet."

Lokie asked the question on everyone's mind. "What does this amulet have to do with her?"

"There was a time when her teacher, a powerful shaman called Letodah, was not happy with Cistoo."

"Why?" This woman shaman intrigued Lokie.

"I'll tell you what, little one. Why don't you wear this amulet around your neck as I share the story. You'll get the most out of it that way. As I recall, the tale goes like this."

Jess described the circumstances of Cistoo's relationship with her father, Euchella. Lokie vividly imagined every detail unfolding before her as she tenderly touched the amulet with her fingertips.

Chapter 13

Cistoo's Trip Back Down the River

Cistoo worried as she set out on the long canoe trip back to visit her father. The outpost lay several miles from where her tribe had previously lived, a level plateau on the mountainside. Cistoo carried enough jerky, corn mush, and bread to last a few weeks. She could catch fish and pick berries along the shore.

While she would be easy to spot on the water, both she and Letodah believed that traveling by water would be safer than by land. She could make better time, and she would be harder to reach—even with a rifle shot. Anyway, an Indian traveling alone presented more of a curiosity than a threat to colonists. Other Indians would not be scared of her. She went in peace but also bore her arrows and her hatchet.

Cistoo took the English paper money that Jane, her white captive, had carried in her satchel. When she first saw the paper money, she thought it was useless; it had pictures on it of English people in funny, fancy clothes. Cistoo did not understand why these odd-looking strips of paper were worth anything, but she believed Jane. Jane had brought the money with her a long distance. *She must have a good reason to do that,* Cistoo thought.

Jane had explained to her, "You can exchange this paper for goods at a trading post. They accept it in trade."

Cistoo's first day on the river was calm, and the river was still. It was a warm day in early spring. The sounds of the birds chirping and the frogs croaking at night created a soothing atmosphere. *The frogs agree with my decision to make this trip,* she thought. She wanted to reach her father soon. She wanted to see him alive. Perhaps love would be the only gift she could give him—and a traditional Cherokee funeral. She would bury him properly, despite the danger.

Uppermost in her mind was the fact that she must not draw attention to herself.

Cistoo estimated four weeks to return to her old village. Letodah told her that the Indian, Nancy, living at the trading post had felt sorry for Euchella and taken him in. Nancy did not want to see one of her own left out on the ground to die alone. She had told one of the shaman's messengers. "I cannot allow such disrespect."

The weather held up well for her, with only two days of rain. The showers had occurred mostly on those nights when she pulled the canoe up to the bank to sleep. Nights were humid. She sweated profusely. Mosquitoes covered her arms and legs. She had dozens of bites.

She was making better time than the group had made on the final trip to Arkansas. Traveling alone simplified the trip. Fewer people equaled fewer illnesses, accidents, mistakes—all those problems had slowed the first group down. Large groups were also slowed by the weakest rower in the crew. Still, with more people, a healthy person could fill in for a sick one. No one could fill in for Cistoo. But she was in excellent shape. She knew what she was doing. She was focused and dedicated to her mission. Nothing short of capture or death would deter her from her goal.

She added miles to her daily distance by letting the canoe drift down the river on its own, while she caught a few hours of sleep. When ashore, she slept fifty to one hundred yards from her canoe, in case a person should spy it. She covered the boat with leaves for camouflage. And her hand tightly gripped the hatchet as she slept. She wanted to have an advantage over any attacker.

Every night when the weather was dry, she journeyed to the Upper World to check on her father's health. *You will find him alive*, the Council of Elders assured her. Yet she did not feel reassured. Letodah had taught her that a shaman's personal desires could block an accurate prediction. No doubt she cared about the outcome in this situation.

My father must still be breathing. He must.

Every day, she dealt with emotions packed down deep inside of her. *How will he react to me now?* She worried. She remembered little about the time before her sixth season, when her father had treated her warmly.

In cases like these, when emotions could influence how she perceived the spiritual advice, she used dreams and stick tossing to verify the elders' message. If the messages matched, she could put more faith in their accuracy.

After two weeks on the river, Cistoo concluded, *I'm getting mixed messages from the spirits. I really can't trust any of them. I care too much about how this turns out.*

Her first big challenge came in the third week, when she had to negotiate the rapids. The rapids were rougher than she'd expected. *I must keep my canoe in one piece.*

Skillfully she worked her oar to miss the rocks. Applying all of her body weight, she shifted the canoe from one direction to another. Making split-second decisions, she got through it mostly unscathed, except for a small hole in the top of her bow and a scrape on her hand. *I'll patch it with mud and leaves when I stop for the night.*

Nearing her destination, she saw the first people—two white women working in a small field, tending to a crop of corn.

When she saw them from a distance, she put on her bonnet and waved. Although they exchanged puzzled glances, the women waved back.

Letodah had gotten the word to the woman who was caring for Euchella, whose name was Nancy, to expect Cistoo's visit. He had sent a series of messengers because he had known Cistoo would return when he told her about her father's condition. Together Cistoo and Letodah had hatched a story. "If you must explain who you are, you will say you are Nancy's sister visiting from the northwest."

Unknown to Cistoo, Letodah had also told Melauki to follow behind her in his own canoe. Just far enough behind so she wouldn't see him. Cistoo would never have voluntarily accepted this protection. *This is my personal journey. I must make it alone. I will not subject anyone else to danger.* Besides, she had trained for her role as a spirit warrior her whole life. She felt confident in her abilities to fend for herself.

She arrived five days faster than it had taken the group to travel upstream. Arriving as the sun set, she walked the distance from her banked canoe until she reached the trading post. A few small, wooden houses sat on the edge of the post. Letodah had told her that she would recognize the house by the goat tied up in the yard and by the cornstalks on the side. When they had lived in their home village, Letodah had taught her a way through the woods into the trading post to avoid detection by the lookouts.

The fire in the fireplace shone through the cabin's tiny window. Cistoo could see Nancy sitting in the corner. She also made out a figure lying on blankets on the floor.

Did he move? She held her breath as she moved closer; she thought she had seen his chest heave. Following Letodah's instructions, she knocked on the door five times, the signal Letodah had messaged Nancy to expect.

The woman came to the door and opened it just enough for Cistoo to fit through and waved for her to come in. Nancy put her index finger to her lips. "Sssh," she whispered. "He is still with us, but he will die soon."

"Has he asked for me?" Cistoo regretted the words as soon as she uttered them. She had to ask, even though she already knew the answer.

Nancy shook her head "no" as if she herself found it hard to believe the response she had to give. Then she added, "But he has been out of his mind from the fever."

I think I would have given up on this man long ago, Nancy thought. *Still, I admire this girl for showing her father such respect—even though he doesn't deserve it.* Euchella was well known at the trading post for his constant drunkenness.

Cistoo walked over to her father and squatted next to him. "I'm here, Father. I came when I heard you were so sick."

Euchella moaned slightly, but his eyes stayed shut.

Knowing she had traveled far, Nancy brought Cistoo a bowl of corn mush. Cistoo devoured several bowls and asked for a third. She licked the bowl and wiped her mouth with her hand.

Cistoo sat next to her father for hours. Long after Nancy had gone to sleep, she gave in to exhaustion. Resting her head on one of the blankets given to her, she covered herself with the other.

She felt her father's head. It was no longer hot; his fever had broken. His blanket was drenched with sweat. She removed the blanket from him and replaced it with the dry blanket she had used to cover herself.

Her father lay stock still the rest of the night. Lying next to him, she slept so lightly that any sound woke her. Several times during the night, she heard him moan. She doubted that she would have slept at all if she had not been so exhausted.

She understood the gravity of the situation: her father would die. Still she felt warmed being so close to him. She had not felt this close to him since she was a small girl. Lying there next to him with their sides touching, she felt the same longing for unfulfilled wishes she had lived with most of her life. Yet she also felt a poignant satisfaction. She enjoyed being so near to him; at last she had the physical closeness she had yearned for. It didn't matter that her feelings were not returned—not that she knew of, anyway.

She knew it was a sacred moment. Although it had been years since she had cried, a tear spilled down her cheek. Quickly she wiped it away. *I cannot allow myself this softness. I have much to do before I can safely return to my people. This is a stop in the road for me, but it is personal. As a shaman, I must remember that my life belongs to my people.*

She would have to be especially cautious on her return trip so that no one would follow her. Leading the enemies of her people back to where they lived was an outcome she must avoid at all costs. She would give her life before she would let that happen.

Briefly, she questioned the wisdom of coming there. *I hope I have done the right thing, putting myself in danger.* Some of her tribes' people thought it was an unnecessary danger. The tribe knew they needed Cistoo, and they were grateful to her; they actually venerated her for all she had done for them. Yet those who had known her since she was a child understood the importance of her trip.

In another way, though, trying to reach a resolution with Euchella would influence the effectiveness of her role as shaman for the rest of her life. She could justify her trip with that fact. She would not have her power held back by unresolved doubts about her relationship with her father. *Even if my father created this distance between us, I have tried many times to approach him.* Yet she still had nagging feelings that maybe there was more she could have done to make him love her.

Maybe I do have true badness at my core that only my father can see. That was her worse thought, but she could not be a powerful shaman and believe that about herself.

But what could have been so bad about me that it made him go away from me forever? If it was because she had infected her mother with a fatal illness, then surely he would know she had no control over that. *I was just a child and never meant to hurt my mother.*

All of these thoughts flew through her mind as she watched her father at dawn. In the daylight, she could see much better. She could see how ashen his face looked. His eyes, rimmed with red, slightly open, were quite yellow. Deep lines crossed his face. On those rare moments when she could see him move, his hands trembled. He groaned. *I know he must feel great pain.* She felt different than she had when she had seen such dire illness in a tribesman. She knew the end was near. All she could do was talk to the spirits. "Please take your brave home, Great Spirit. Spare him pain."

She used medicinal plants she carried with her to stave off the agony. She felt helpless and hopeless with Euchella, despite the pain-calming plants.

"You may not be able to hear me, Father, but I am here." She wiped his forehead with cool water from her host's bucket. "I am here." She held his hand.

Nancy woke up and went about her morning chores. Out of respect for Cistoo, she did not disturb this sacred time of dying. Dying was a journey back to the sky vault home. Soon Euchella's spirit would rejoin the ancestors who had gone before him.

Cistoo sat for hours—her hand on top of her father's hand. Sometimes she closed her eyes in prayer, but mostly she looked at him. *He looks so small and helpless lying there.* He was not at all the huge, looming character who had dominated her heart and mind for so many years.

Nancy quietly interrupted her to give her food. The host then spent her day outside tending to the corn, vegetables, and milking the goat. With any luck, Cistoo's visit would be brief and go completely unnoticed by others at the trading post.

Euchella's breath grew shallower. At one point, he opened his eyes slightly. When he opened his mouth to speak, his voice was so weak Cistoo could barely hear him. Bending over his face, she put her ear next to his lips. He said the word twice, so she knew she had understood it correctly. "Daughter ... daughter."

Cistoo's heart leaped for joy. She had not heard her father call her by any name for twenty years. Then his eyes closed, and his breathing got shallower and less frequent. She heard a gurgling sound inside his throat. She had heard that sound before, so she knew what to expect. He would die very soon.

She remembered the time he had sung a lullaby to help her sleep. *Do you know how beautiful you are? It's like looking up at a bright and shiny star in the black expanse of night.*

When Nancy came back into the house to prepare the midday meal she, too, could see that Euchella lay close to the end.

"If I give you some money, could you dig a hole for his burial?" Cistoo asked. "We must put a mound on top. His body must face north. If the hole is deep enough, we will not have to worry about dogs or wolves digging his body up and tearing it apart."

Nancy was glad to get the money. She had rarely had money. It would come in handy, especially during the winter when supplies ran low. She put up food from the garden and she hunted, but hunting was never 100 percent reliable. Some seasons' game was more plentiful than others'.

Cistoo sat and watched her father intently. Several minutes had passed since he had taken a breath. She might have thought it was over, except that he had been breathing at that pace for about an hour.

Cistoo was praying for him to have safe passage into the Galvladi tsosv when an intuition came to her. She removed the turquoise amulet that Letodah had given her when she had first become a shaman. She felt Letodah would understand. No one else knew better than he did how much she had suffered because of her father's shunning.

She placed the amulet around Euchella's neck. "May the power of this amulet heal the suffering of your life and guide you peacefully to your ancestors."

Euchella took two more breaths after Cistoo gave him the blessing; then he died.

She was not overcome with grief—or any other emotion, for that matter. *I am thankful I was here for you, Father.*

Cistoo could not afford to linger. As soon as night fell, she scanned the environment to be certain the area was clear. Then she and Nancy carried Euchella's body, wrapped in a blanket, to the freshly dug grave. The two carefully lowered his body so that his head faced north, just as Euchella had done twenty years earlier for Cistoo's mother. This ritual protected future relatives from contracting a painful bone disease.

The dirt was packed over the body, leaving a slightly rounded mound.

"Thank you, Nancy. I am very grateful." She gave her host the money she had promised. *I wish I could have buried him next to my mother, but she is not near enough.*

Cistoo had communicated with Nancy in English, and she realized how valuable her lessons with Jane had been. For the first time since she had left she thought of Jane. She looked forward to learning more when she returned.

Cistoo set out into the woods. She had been at the trading post less than a full day. The shorter the stay, the better the chance of her remaining undetected. Luckily, no one had come by the house during her brief time there. Moonlight guided her through the woods. Her plan was to find her canoe and make her way upstream toward home. She needed to put distance between herself and the trading post as soon as possible, for safety's sake. She had gotten little sleep.

As she neared the canoe, she heard the signal she and Melauki alone shared. *Melauki must be near. What is he doing here?* she thought. Then she saw him approaching.

"Let's row back together. I can row while you sleep," he said.

Cistoo wanted to ask him why he had followed her. *Isn't it clear that I can do this by myself? I don't need you.* But she didn't have the energy to argue. She was glad that he was there.

Epilogue

unt Jess lived to be one hundred years old. And she had a new story to tell her great-grandchildren. It was a story about how a young girl named Lokie had made a big discovery that helped her tribe learn more about their history. Lokie learned about a young Indian shaman girl from another century. A modern-day storyteller named Andross wrote the story, and it was published in an important magazine. When folks read it, they wanted to meet Lokie. A number of people sent her money for her education. She studied history at the University of North Carolina, uncovering new facts about Cherokee women in North Carolina history. Now she teaches those stories to her students.

When Lokie comes home on the weekends, she attends the Church of the Living Vine with her grandmother, Johnny Jay, and the crewmembers who moved the relatives carefully from one cemetery to another.